HOW TO READ
HOUSES

HOW TO READ
HOUSES

A crash course in domestic architecture

Will Jones

Herbert Press
An imprint of Bloomsbury Publishing Plc

H E R B E R T   P R E S S
LONDON · OXFORD · NEW YORK · NEW DELHI · SYDNEY

Herbert Press

An imprint of Bloomsbury Publishing Plc

50 Bedford Square	1385 Broadway
London	New York
WC1B 3DP	NY 10018
UK	USA

www.bloomsbury.com

**BLOOMSBURY and the Diana logo are
trademarks of Bloomsbury Publishing Plc**

First published in Great Britain in
2013 by Bloomsbury Publishing Plc

Reprinted in 2014, 2015, 2016, 2017

© 2017 Quarto Publishing plc

British Library Cataloguing-in-Publication Data

A catalogue record for this book is available from the
British Library.

ISBN: 978-1-9122-1711-3

Printed in China

This book was conceived, designed
and produced by

Ivy Press

An imprint of The Quarto Group
The Old Brewery, 6 Blundell Street
London N7 9BH, United Kingdom
T (0)20 7700 6700 **F** (0)20 7700 8066

www.QuartoKnows.com

CREATIVE DIRECTOR Peter Bridgewater
PUBLISHER Jason Hook
EDITORIAL DIRECTOR Caroline Earle
ART DIRECTOR Michael Whitehead
SENIOR EDITOR Stephanie Evans
DESIGN JC Lanaway
ILLUSTRATOR Sandra Pond

Contents

There are many different types of building, from cathedrals and skyscrapers to toll booths and bus shelters, but none is more familiar than the house, the very place in which we live. However, while we travel to see architectural icons and while tourist guides are emblazoned with images of the most prestigious or historic structures, little attention is paid to the design of the house, unless it is an architect's fantasy splashed across the pages of a design magazine. Yet almost every house has been designed according to an architectural style or a number of styles. Its size, shape, layout, features and decoration either overtly express a specific architectural movement or give clues as to the style that the architect was inspired by when designing it. Houses tell the human story of architecture better than any other type of building.

Moreover, the design of houses has been influenced by the nationality of architects and builders ever since medieval times. Architectural nuances can be identified and traced back to a

Thoroughly Modernist
Le Corbusier's Villa Savoye, a country house in Poissy, northeast of Paris, France, has defining traits. The long, thin 'ribbon' windows, flat roof and slender, undecorated columns are all hallmarks of a Modernist design.

specific country or settlement. For instance, America was colonised predominantly by Europeans who brought with them their traditional building techniques – the colonial styles. However, over time these individual national styles blended (as did the settlers) and a new American colonial architectural style was born.

But what drove master builders and architects, and what inspires designers today, to create houses in different styles, to forgo or follow architectural fashions? The answers are many and varied but they are almost always visible in the design of a house and, with a little insight, are easy to spot.

Take the two houses pictured. The flamboyance of Mark Twain House puts it completely at odds with the near-clinical austerity of Villa Savoye, which shuns extravagant gesture in favour of functionality. And there's the key, the elements that mark each house as different from another. The

Victorian, with Gothic elements
The roof pitch, style and placement of the windows, the stickwork and decoration tell us that Mark Twain House in Hartford, USA, is Victorian, with a splash of Gothic thrown in.

clues are all there. They may not be as immediately evident as on these two archetypes but look carefully and even the most unremarkable house will begin to reveal its style and design history. The trick is knowing what to look for – this book will set you on the road to becoming a real residential architecture sleuth.

Looking for Clues

Learning to read the clues that reveal a building's style is not like learning mathematics; there can be definitive answers but more often than not, as the word 'style' suggests, you are looking for some sort of hint, or trait, that gives up part of the answer. Take the two houses pictured below, a Victorian townhouse and a Prairie-style suburban home. While both have similar features – doors, windows, pitched roofs etc – they are very different. The upright style of the Victorian house contrasts with the low horizontal lines of the Prairie-style home. Roof overhangs are larger on the Prairie home. The Victorian has bay windows, plus decorative effects, while the Prairie design uses form rather than fanciful flourish to illustrate its character.

Victorian style
The Victorian era brought out the extravagance in architects following a period of restraint, when Georgian design had ruled. Bay windows of different sizes began to appear, coloured brickwork and decorative roof edge detailing all announced the arrival of a new architectural style.

Prairie style
In America the geography of the country and abundance of land profoundly affected the shape of houses, spreading as they did horizontally rather than upwards. Prairie-style architects accentuated this with low-pitched roofs and long balconies, creating large but seemingly ground-hugging houses.

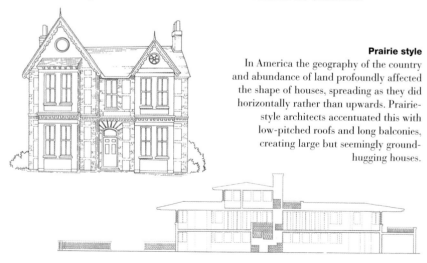

Quirky traits

Why build such fancy chimney stacks? Because, in Tudor times, the enclosed fireplace was a new invention and being able to afford a house with one was a status symbol. Owners signalled their wealth from the roofs of their houses and what finer way to do it than with this flamboyant architectural statement?

Old on new

Much design takes reference from history and architecture is no exception. Here, a relatively new timber-framed house is stylised with the addition of columns and a pediment on its front façade. The four round columns and decorative triangular pediment turn a normal 1960s house into a Neoclassical home.

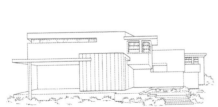

Style giveaways

Some design elements are so specific to a particular style that they are instantly recognisable. Here, the long 'ribbon' window is a giveaway, marking this house as one of Modernist design. The lack of a visible window frame is also a trademark of Modernism.

Oddities

There are always exceptions to the rule and here a century-old farmhouse (with pitched roof) has been extended with a Modernist addition. The contrast is immediately evident, but with good design, as in this case, the mixing of very different styles can be made to work.

Introduction

Simple splendour
Casa das Canoas, designed by Oscar Niemeyer, is the Brazilian architect's Modernist interpretation of a single-storey house. This simple home shuns decoration in favour of using architectural elements, such as the extended roof beams and large glazed openings, to make a dramatic statement.

Houses come in many shapes and sizes depending upon their location, style, the materials available and the inhabitants they are built for. This is what makes residential architecture such a rich subject to explore.

While style traits give clues as to the architectural fashion of an era, the size and extravagance of a house also provide valuable information as to the occupants. For instance, a detached Victorian townhouse would likely have the same style of window as a terraced row of Victorian workers' houses. The two residences would be vastly different in scale but no matter, everyone of that era, rich or poor, aspired to the same style.

Houses often take their cue from the landscape surrounding them. This can mean low-slung horizontal lines that work well in an open flat prairie or row after row of compact houses designed to house hundreds of workers close to a large factory. Similarly, the opulence of the owner is often expressed in terms of size, whether that is multiple storeys in a large Georgian villa, a sprawling single floor Ranch-style house or an apartment set within a grand block that is disguised as a single large house. Reading architecture is as much about reading people and their aspirations as tracing a style or movement.

Top-notch terraces

Terraces come in many forms. People often associate them with small houses in impoverished parts of cities. However, some of the most prestigious addresses are also terraces. For example, Park Crescent in central London is a grand Georgian terrace designed by architect John Nash.

Multi-Storey Houses

The mansion
Designed by French architect René Moreau, Maison Mantin is an eccentric villa built for Louis Mantin, a wealthy businessman from Moulins in central France. The style is a mix of Gothic and Renaissance, creating an almost fairytale aesthetic that harks back to earlier and much larger château architecture in France.

Multi-storey houses are probably the most common of all house types because they provide plenty of living space on a compact site. This means that more of them can be built on a given area than their single-storey equivalents. Building upwards was initially a challenge but by Tudor times two- and three-storey houses were being constructed, and by the 17th century well-to-do urban dwellings often had four or five floors, including the basement, with the main floors being used by the family, and uppermost and lower ones by servants. Today, such houses are often split into apartments and most single, multi-storey houses have just two floors.

One-and-a-half-storey

This rural Canadian cottage is typical of houses built in the area in the 19th century. The dormer window above the main door supplements light to the upper floor, in addition to windows in the gable ends of the house. The dormer trim is Gothic in style, while the windows and door on the lower floor reveal Georgian influence.

Three-storey townhouse

Built at the end of a terrace of similar properties, this three-storey townhouse was, and still is, a common sight in British towns and cities. Big enough for a family but not too large for the average professional to afford, it was the house of choice for many. This example is Georgian in style, as can be deduced by the restrained nature of the design.

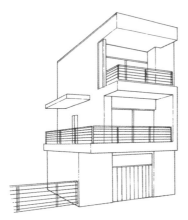

Duplex

The duplex refers to a single building that houses two homes in the same property; typically, a first-floor apartment with another above it. Here, a contemporary duplex has all the hallmarks of Modernist design, its clean lines and minimal porch bereft of unnecessary decoration. The lowest storey is a parking garage.

Single-Storey Houses

A singular storey
Designed in 1949 by renowned US architect Philip Johnson, the Glass House in New Canaan, Connecticut is an exercise in the distillation of modernism. The small dwelling is completely transparent except for a central pod to house the bathroom. While not practical in most circumstances, the house represents the refinement of living requirements, so aspired to by Modernists.

Single-storey houses require, in most cases, more space on which to be built than their multi-storey counterparts and as such they tend to be found in suburban and rural areas. A fine example of this is in the USA, where, having no spatial confinements, architects designed vast suburbs of Ranch-style houses, each with a yard all around – the 'perfect' family home model. In other countries, single-storey dwellings tend to be small and are often built as retirement homes. The lack of stairs is a boon for the elderly, who also require less space than a growing family. There are of course exceptions, as exemplified by the Glass House, designed by Philip Johnson for his own use, pictured below.

Ranch style

Often L- or U-shaped with an open-plan interior, Ranch-style houses became very popular in the USA in the 1940s and 50s. The simple design of these houses adopts Modernist ideals but softens them by reference to the traditional ranches of the Midwest. The result is a long, low style with the horizontal emphasis accentuated by the wide overhang of the eaves.

English bungalow

The quintessential English bungalow is a small house, typically with symmetrical windows around a central front door and a low-pitched, hipped roof (as shown above). The house contained two bedrooms at most, making it a modest property, perfect for the relative scarcity of land in England.

Earthship

As individuals become increasingly conscious of their impact upon the planet, they design houses differently. This earthship is built into a hillside to give it extra insulation, while its southerly aspect is glazed to capture the sun's warmth. Building high involves more financial costs than limiting the construction to a single storey; building using the earth has long-term residual benefits.

New ideas

Los Andes House in Peru by Juan Carlos Doblado is a stunning example of a new single-storey house. One part of it is built into the Andean foothills, while the other is elevated above the ground, apparently unsupported. This illusion makes use of a cantilever – the 'floating' portion of the dwelling is supported by the grounded element.

Attached Houses

Creole townhouses, such as these, were erected after the Great New Orleans Fire of 1788 until the mid-19th century. The terraces are built up to the property line and have wrought-iron balconies that extend out over the pavement. The style, while not unique to New Orleans, is a city tourist attraction nonetheless.

Efficiencies of scale can be applied to many things, including houses. Indeed, space-saving measures are often paramount when houses are built in rows or terraces. Since the industrial revolution, workers have been housed in small homes next to their place of work. These homes were planned in rows – back to back – packed close together. Conversely, grand terraces of more upmarket urban areas were popular in Georgian times: architectural spectacles incorporating parks and royal crescents. Such terraces often had Classical elements, including Greek Revival columns and pediments, to heighten the extravagance.

Houses for workers

Rows of workers' houses were typical of many industrial towns in northern England during the industrial revolution. The small houses offered scant space for large families but poorly paid workers were thankful for this job-tied accommodation as opposed to the squalor of city slums.

Royal row houses

Lansdown Crescent in Bath, England is a fine example of an upper-class Georgian terrace. Built in the late 18th century and designed by John Palmer, the crescent is restrained in a repeating design except at its centre, where four large pilasters rise to a Classical-style triangular pediment.

Canadian oddity

Standing on Rue Sherbrooke East in Montreal, Canada, these unusual terraced houses are evidence of the excesses of architectural freedom. The rusticated façades of the houses are outdone by an extravagant roof detailing that crams in every type of Neoclassical feature possible, and then repeats it again and again.

Tudor masquerade

This stand-alone mock-Tudor house is in fact two 19th-century cottages designed to look like a single dwelling. Unusual as this is, the idea of joining together two homes, as semi-detached houses, is not uncommon. Here, however, the unknown architect/ builder has taken it a step further and disguised the two houses as one.

Detached Houses

Modern ideals

The American architect Richard Neutra designed the Kaufmann Desert House in 1946. The five-bedroom house is set in its own grounds in Palm Springs, California. Neutra's design requires the occupants to circulate both internally and externally to move around the house's many rooms.

Standing alone, within its own property and surrounded by a fortification of lawn and picket fence, this is the filmic view of the detached house – the working man's castle. In reality, the detached house can take many forms and throughout architectural history it has been the platform for experimentation on which architects have tested their theories and fancies. The size of a detached house can vary greatly, from a 30-bedroom French château to a single living space housed within round wooden poles set in the Canadian wilderness. Both qualify as a detached house purely by the fact that they are not joined to another.

Tudor magnificence

With its timber-framed walls and steeply pitched roofs, plus high ornamented chimney stacks, this Tudor mansion is as grand as houses got in the 16th century.

The building would have represented a major undertaking at the time of its construction, when master builders, rather than architects, took responsibility for building such houses.

Neoclassical villa

Neoclassical design is not restricted to a particular era but is about the use of particular stylistic elements. Here, Romanesque arches and Classical columns are contrasted with simple rectangular windows and even Hispanic detailing at cornice level, an unusual mix but one that works.

Colonial dwelling

Built to serve as a home and a school house, the Voorlezer's House is a 17th-century Dutch Colonial house in Richmond Town, New York. The timber construction and small windows were typical of the period. The house was home to the minister and was therefore a prestigious dwelling in a new settlement.

Apartments

A living legacy
Unité d'Habitation is a housing scheme in Marseilles, France. Designed by Modernist architect Le Corbusier, it was envisaged as a city within itself, where residents of varied backgrounds and social status could mix and share the facilities that included on-site shops, a doctor, communal child care and sports facilities (there is a running track on the roof).

Mass-housing schemes are a relatively new addition to residential architecture when you consider that humankind has been making homes since Neolithic times. Most large-scale residential buildings are multi-storey and so were difficult and expensive to build before the time of concrete and steel. Today, however, a great many people share the building in which they live with other occupants. And, as populations grow and urban areas become more crowded, houses will get smaller and more concentrated. This concentration of homes comes in two forms – newly built projects and adaptations of existing, sometimes historic, buildings. Each type offers different advantages, depending upon your preference for a crisp new living space or the charm of living in a piece of architectural history.

Condominium

The condominium is a building housing numerous apartments, which occupants either lease or buy. However, due to the collective nature of these apartments, residents share services and the costs of the building's upkeep. There is no difference between a condominium and an apartment building, other than the form of ownership.

The high life

One of most prestigious addresses in Manhattan, New York, 8 Spruce Street is a residential tower designed by Frank Gehry. Its construction is indicative of the growing need for more high-class housing in cities. Until recently, the vast majority of residential towers were built in less wealthy neighbourhoods and reserved for working-class families.

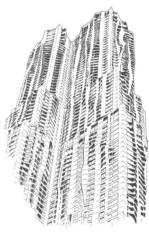

Masquerading as houses

Originally designed, by architect F. L. Bonfoey, as a 1920s family home in Charlotte, North Carolina, for the Rutzlers, this Neoclassical mansion has since been adapted to house 18 separate apartments. More and more often this is the fate of large historic urban houses, which once stood on the edge of cities but have now been swallowed up within the city limits.

Introduction

The type of material that a house is built from depends upon several factors. What type of construction is the building? What size is the building? Which materials are available? Which materials are affordable? What style of design is the building? The list goes on.

Historically, materials were less numerous and so an overriding aesthetic usually formed depending first and foremost upon geographic location and then style. For instance, Tudor houses were generally timber framed with infill panels of wattle and daub because wood was plentiful as was the mud and branches needed to make wattle and daub. This style of construction allows for easy recognition of Tudor buildings. Today there are a plethora of different materials available, from stone and earth to solar-absorbing glass and all manner of plastics.

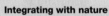

Integrating with nature
Building within a beautiful natural setting is challenging. Few houses can be totally hidden, so a harmonious design must be achieved. Frank Lloyd Wright's Fallingwater in Bear Run, Pennsylvania, successfully blends reinforced concrete with the rock strata of the waterfall to create one of Modernism's most enduring and exciting house designs.

With the proliferation of materials and their use within all manner of architectural styles, the identification of those different styles demands the ability to look past the materials and spot other design traits. However, that does not make materials any less important in reading houses.

For instance, the architects of many new Modernist houses in Canada still tend towards using materials that echo the local past and appeal to clients. Wood and stone are still used where other newer materials could be substituted. They may even cloak a high-tech façade, hiding the true design innovations from view. This may be a difficult choice for the architect but one made to please the client. The result of such design trickery is the development of a new local vernacular, a connection with history and location even though the architecture is thoroughly contemporary.

Ease and availability
Locally available and familiar materials that could be worked by skilled craftsmen are factors that explain why reed and stone were used for the design and construction of the Arts and Crafts-influenced Happisburgh Manor in Norfolk, England. Its architect, Detmar Jellings Blow, chose the thatched roof and flint and pebble wall treatment as much for their availability as their wonderful look.

Stone

Stone is one of the oldest and most versatile building materials. Houses have been carved from it, constructed of it and decorated with it since people gained the skills to work this hardwearing material. The type of stone used to build houses in the past usually depended upon what was available locally because, due to its weight, stone was, and still is, difficult and expensive to transport. However, as a structural building material it is one of the strongest and most reliable – since medieval times foundations and walls have been built of stone, due to its load-bearing capacity. Today, while concrete is cheaper, stone continues to be favoured, whether in structural form or as a cladding material, over less costly wall construction.

Old world charm
Reputedly the oldest standing structure in Georgetown, Washington, DC, the Old Stone House was built in 1765. It is a prime example of colonial architecture, but became very run down in the early part of the 20th century. Happily, it was restored to its original condition in the 1950s by the US National Park Service.

Traditional stone

These Italian mountain dwellings are typical of traditional stone construction the world over. Slabs of local stone have been roughly cut and shaped before being stacked, with no binding agent, to create walls. Although the method is rudimentary, the skill to build supporting walls that were stable is one learned over years of practice.

Contemporary stone

The inherent strength and thermal properties of stone are used to good effect in this contemporary house in Bosnia, by DVA Arhitekta. Thick walls are strong and they also regulate the internal temperature of the building, reducing the need for mechanical heating and cooling.

Mediterranean stone

This French house is not old but it has been built using traditional techniques and styles. The dry stone walls are of local stone and the wooden trellis is indicative of Mediterranean houses – its purpose is to support grape vines, which provide fruit and shade to the occupants.

Brick

Dating back to at least 7500 BC, the earliest bricks found were little more than shaped mud blocks, which were dried in the sun. These provided the building medium for the ancient civilisations of, for example, Mesopotamia and Pakistan. However, since firing techniques were developed, the brick has become one of the most enduring of all building materials. Laid in courses (of which there are many styles and patterns) and bonded with a variety of materials, from lime to cement and even glue, bricks provide a strong, load-bearing outer façade for a house. To be able to create level courses, bricks have to be made of equal size and so countries have developed standards for brick sizes. Surprisingly, these differ quite significantly.

Best of brick
Dating from 1540, this Dutch house, which is now home to the Edam Museum, features a wonderfully decorative stepped brick gable. The versatile material enabled builders to create impressive structures and patterns relatively easily, so endearing brick to architects right through to the present day.

Common or American

English

Running

English cross or Dutch

Bonding patterns

Courses of bricks are laid one on top of the other to form walls. Bonding patterns make the composition and structure uniform while maximising strength and visual appeal. Brick size varies considerably: Russia and Sweden use a standard of 250 × 120 × 65 mm (10 × 4¾ × 2½ in) bricks, whereas the size in the UK is 215 × 102.5 × 65 mm (8½ × 4 × 2¼ in).

Combining techniques

This half-timbered English house has brickwork infill rather than conventional wattle and daub. The reason for this quirk is unknown but what it illustrates is the versatility of construction materials such as wood and bricks, and the ingenuity of the craftspeople who use them.

Modern use of brick

By using extremely dense engineering bricks, the designer of this contemporary house has created an unusual and dramatic building. Engineering bricks are more costly than conventional ones and less porous: they are generally used only on the lower courses of houses, where the wall is more likely to come into prolonged contact with wet ground.

Wood

Wonderful wood
This 16th-century wool merchant's house in the east of England has a timber frame. But look at the window frames, panelled doors, cornice and horizontal beam: all wood, worked with great skill, to turn a simple house into one of real beauty.

Wood has always been an important structural material in many house types across the globe. Its strength and the ease with which it can be worked also make wood one of the most versatile materials. From the great Tudor houses to aboriginal longhouses and pioneers' cabins to the beauty of the Arts and Crafts-inspired architecture and intricate gingerbread tracery, wood has always been in fashion. Today, the material's benefits include the fact that it is an environmentally friendly resource that can be produced in many forms: timbers, laminated beams, particle boards, insulation. Wood is perhaps the most widely used building material in the world.

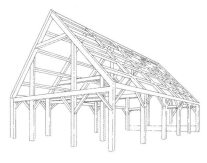

Classic log cabin

This cabin uses entire tree trunks, scraped of their bark. Hewn from the vast forests of evergreens in North America, the logs are lapped at the corners with simple half- round joints, making a strong, stable structure. The design is centuries-old and houses are still built using these methods.

Timber-framed house

The post-and-beam structure of a timber-framed house gives strength and beauty to the finished home. Heavy 15–30-cm (6–12-in) timbers are joined with pegged mortise and tenon joints and can be erected quite quickly. An outer skin is built over the frame to protect it; this can be of similar natural materials or any manner of new high-performance façade.

Structural timber panels

The advent of plywood and wooden particle board panels has meant architects and contractors are able to build framed walls and roof elements and then piece them together like a giant jigsaw puzzle to form a house. This is one of the most common building techniques used in North America today, due to its speed and relative low cost compared with other techniques.

Modern wooden houses

Architects José Ulloa Davet and Delphine Ding renovated this Chilean beach house using almost nothing but wood. Both inside and externally, the house is clad in timber slats (to aerate the building and protect it from moisture) and its structural frame is also wood. The result is a beautiful home with a unique visual appeal, one that could not be achieved with any other material.

Concrete

Form and function

Concrete is extremely strong, but its liquid nature when mixed means it is very easily moulded into almost any shape. Architects such as Jergen H. Mayer take advantage of this property to create houses like this one, the Dupli Casa near Ludwigsburg, Germany. The possibilities are limited only by structural constraints, which are overcome by a different concrete mix and steel reinforcing.

Although concrete is thought of as a relatively new material, it has in fact been used since ancient times. The Romans built many impressive buildings using a mixture of quicklime, volcanic ash (or *pozzolana*) and pumice aggregate. However, without steel-reinforcing, concrete had little tensile strength and it wasn't until this was introduced that the true benefits of concrete were discovered. Today, it is considered a multi-faceted building material, as much for its inherent thermal properties (its ability to retain a stable temperature) as its load-bearing qualities. Whether you want a cool house in a hot country or a warm house in a cold one, concrete walls help regulate internal temperatures, reducing the need for costly heating or cooling.

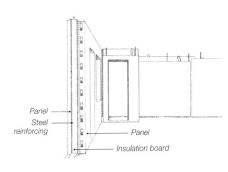

Panel
Steel reinforcing
Panel
Insulation board

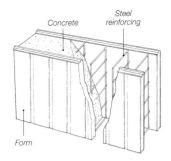

Steel reinforcing
Concrete
Form

Precast panel construction

Concrete construction takes two forms, precast and in situ. Here, precast concrete panels, which have been manufactured off site, are erected to form the load-bearing walls of a house. The panels include steel reinforcing within the set concrete as well as insulation between the internal and external skins.

Poured concrete construction

Concrete can be poured wet into moulds at the site of the house build. Called 'forms', or 'form work', the moulds are built from wood, metal or insulating foam (seen here) and steel reinforcing is secured within them. Concrete is then poured into the moulds and allowed to set hard. Steel or wooden moulds are then removed but these expanded foam ones are left on to provide an insulating layer.

Early concrete houses

Thomas Edison (who some claim invented the light bulb) saw the potential of concrete and founded the Edison Portland Cement Company in 1899. He designed and built this concrete house. At the time his designs for formwork were so expensive that the construction was not economical, and the houses were never built in great numbers.

Modern concrete house

Japanese architect Tadao Ando designs in concrete. Most of his buildings, from houses to churches, are grey boxes and also Minimalist masterpieces. Here, in the 4x4 House in Akashi, Japan, he takes the idea of stacked cubes and shifts one to create a thought-provoking house, built entirely out of concrete.

Metal

MATERIALS

Modernism and metal
Eames House, the Los Angeles home of designers Charles and Ray Eames, is a classic example of steel used as the main structural material for a Modernist house. Left exposed inside and out, the steel frame wall is infilled with solid and glazed panels, and the roof is corrugated steel sheets laid over lightweight lattice beams.

Metal is a relatively new construction material but one that drastically altered the architectural landscape. Suddenly, in the late 19th century, steel frames enabled architects to design extremely tall buildings – the first steel-frame skyscraper was built in Chicago in 1885. The same heavy beams used in skyscraper design can be used in residential construction and were favoured by Modernists, or much smaller section columns and cross members can be erected, much like timber framing, as the load-bearing structure for house walls. This technique became quite common until the cost of steel soared in the early 21st century and now steel's environmental credentials are also being challenged.

Conventional steel framed house

Here, a house that looks like any other brick-built house from the outside, has a steel structural frame. Large rolled-steel beams and columns make up the load-bearing structure, while smaller section pressed-steel columns are used like timber studs to fix plasterboard to, in order to partition off rooms within the house.

Prefabricated metal house

The Dymaxion House, designed by R. Buckminster Fuller, was a factory-manufactured steel house first made in 1929. Fuller wanted to create low-cost, easily erectable houses and based his Dymaxion on the design of a grain bin. Fuller's prefab houses were sent to US troops stationed in the Persian Gulf during the Second World War.

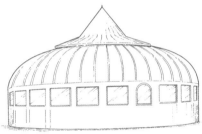

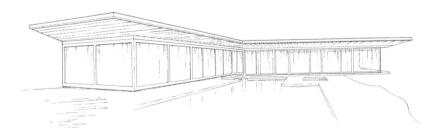

Modernist steel frame

The Case Study Houses were experimental affordable homes designed by top architects in the 1940s, 50s and 60s. Here, the Stahl House in Los Angeles, by Pierre Koenig, uses the slimmest of steel columns and beams to support a sheet steel roof. The effect is a lightness of architecture that transcended the low-cost idealism of the design, and a house that is now world famous.

Adobe

Spanish colonial adobe
California is home to a large number of adobe houses due to its warm climate. This one has a stucco (rendered) finish to its adobe brick walls, giving good insulation in summer and winter. Classic red tiles and the horseshoe archway are traits indicative of a Spanish colonial design. The stucco wall finish can be white or coloured in natural earth tones.

Used predominantly in South America, the sunnier states of North America, Africa and Asia, adobe is a remarkably strong yet incredibly easy and inexpensive building material. Combining sand, clay and water, then adding fibrous material such as grass, sticks or straw, adobe builders press the resulting sticky mix into rectangular wooden frames and let it dry and harden in the sun to make adobe bricks. This base building material is then laid in the same way as conventional bricks, bonded with a mortar of sand, clay and water but no fibrous material. The result is a very strong wall with great thermal properties, making it especially useful for keeping building interiors cool.

Adobe brick wall

Adobe bricks are formed in moulds, tamped down to ensure the raw materials are packed in, and then baked dry in the sun. Once dry they are extremely hard and can be used to build conventional walls, being bonded by lime mortar or mud.

Super adobe

This relatively new version of adobe construction is gaining popularity with sustainable movements. It uses bags or tubes, filled with sand, crushed rock or even rice husks, stacked to create walls (often in a conical or igloo-type shape). The structure is then plastered to provide added insulation and water tightness. The result is a quickly erected and inexpensive house.

Pueblo revival house

Adobe has long been used to construct Pueblo houses, both old and new. They are easily recognisable, having flat roofs, with heavy timbers extending through the walls, stuccoed walls with rounded corners, and deep window reveals, providing a unique style, which may have Spanish colonial twists added, depending upon the location.

Straw

Straw experimentation
It may look a little too simple to be true but this single-pitched house is built entirely out of straw. The material acts both as the main infill/panel element of the wall and also as a great insulator. Spaces are left in the straw walls for doors and windows. The roof sits on timber pads on top of the straw wall.

Straw, grass, reeds and other similar natural materials have been used in construction for thousands of years, but building load-bearing structures with straw bales did not become common until very recently. Environmental issues have helped to promote straw bale construction and as more houses (and other structures) are built, the benefits of straw are becoming more evident. Believe it or not, a straw bale house is more fire-resistant than a wooden one. It will also stand up to an earthquake better than a brick structure. Moreover, the insulation provided by a one-bale-thick wall far outstrips that of the conventional cavity wall of an average British house. Straw is an old material but it is only just beginning to be exploited to full advantage within the construction industry.

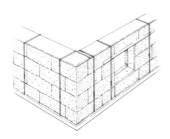

Straw bale construction

The conventional way of building with straw bales is very simple. Set on a timber base plate, the rows of bales are stacked in much the same way as bricks are laid. Wooden stakes are driven into the bales to hold them together, and, where a door or window is required, a heavy load-bearing timber supports the bales above it. Finally, a coat of lime plaster provides a weatherproof skin.

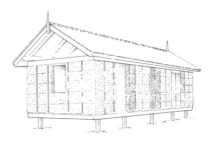

Simple straw bale house

A rectangular construction of bales, stacked in alternating courses on an elevated floor slab, will ensure this simple house is well insulated and warm inside due to the thickness and density of the bales that form the walls.

Traditional straw bale house

Traditional in design, this house in Colorado, USA, has all the usual design elements of a conventional dwelling – roof, windows, doors and so forth. Perhaps the only clue that it could be made of straw is the curved corner detail of the external rendered wall. This is typical of straw bale construction as it is tricky to make sharp corners.

Contemporary straw bale house

This timber-clad house, ultra-modern in appearance, is built using straw bales. The house has a timber frame and outer façade but the main infill material for the walls is straw. This neatly illustrates that straw bale houses don't have to look rustic, and they can be adapted to suit any environment, rural or urban.

Recycled Materials

The reuse or recycling of material is more often than not far better from an environmental perspective than the manufacture of a new one; and this goes for building products just as it does for plastic bottles. In fact, some houses are now made out of plastic bottles. Reuse and recycling take many forms: from innovative ideas such as developing building systems with alternative or waste materials to the reuse of existing items, such as timber from packing crates or blast furnace slag as an aggregate in concrete. The possibilities are limitless and as yet mostly untapped, but as sustainability becomes a bigger issue, people will experiment and innovate to create homes using an ever wider material palette, some of which will be recycled.

Box clever

This unusual live/work cluster in the docklands area of Tower Hamlets in London's East End is one of a number of container cities that have sprung up around the world. Shipping containers provide stable, secure building blocks for construction projects – and there are thousands of them that have outlived their use in the shipping industry.

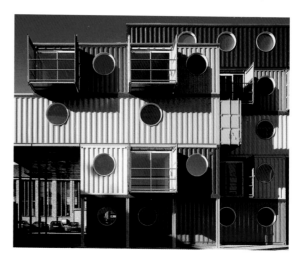

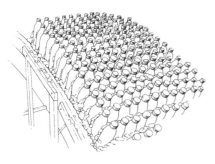

Reclaimed wood

This timber house in the Yukon looks like a well-designed contemporary house. It is, but it is also constructed from reclaimed wood. Flooring and framing timbers are from an old army barracks. The ceiling beams and internal columns are from a demolished mill and the siding was once part of a local warehouse. Builder Mark Berube estimates the cost at around one third of the equivalent in new materials.

Reusing plastic bottles

Filled with sand, waste plastic bottles make a surprisingly insulative building material. They can be either laid on a bed of wet mortar or simply strung together, before being covered in a plaster finish. In both instances they are strong and durable and have surprising insulation value – the air inside maintaining a relatively constant temperature. Plastic bottles have been touted as a material to help solve housing crises in third world countries.

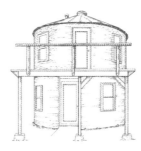

Recycled glass

Waste glass can be converted into glass beads that are then used to manufacture modular panels, used to build houses. This is at the innovative end of recycling and an industry in its infancy, but constructors can now build environmentally friendly homes that look and feel like the conventional houses we are more familiar with.

Recycled grain bin

Taking an old building and converting it is perhaps one of the most sustainable options because you are reusing existing materials. Old churches, warehouses and barns are common renovation projects but here an enterprising individual has converted an old grain bin to create a unique cylindrical house.

Slate (covering)

MATERIALS

Wall shingles
This Queen Anne-style house, built by architect Frederick Schock for himself in Austin, Texas, features great use of a number of materials, from the rough-cut stone walls and detailed patinated copper trim, to the expanse of slate wall shingles which adorn the upper storeys and the roof.

Slate tiles or shingles are a traditional roof covering in various areas of the UK, where the stone is extracted locally. It is also used in Brazil, Newfoundland (Canada) and the east coast of the USA, from Maine down to Virginia. Slate is suitable for building due to its very low water absorption and its natural tendency to split into smooth flat sheets when struck with specialist tools. It can be used either for thin roof tiles or in thicker slabs suitable for building walls. Slate also makes good floor tiles and headstones. Entire villages in Wales are crowned with slate roofs, making for wonderful views of 'local' architecture.

New slate design

Haus Köhler is a renovated German house, by Bruno Blesch. Clad entirely in precision-cut slate tiles, the house is a new take on a classic covering. The slate is long lasting and provides good thermal stability, reducing temperature fluctuations and moderating the environment inside throughout the year.

Roof covering

Victorian architects often used slate, in part because of its availability but also because it contrasted well with the red brick which they favoured. Here, an octagonal roof features both conventional slate tiles and a fishscale pattern, added purely for decorative effect.

Slate all over

Located at St Fagans, the National History Museum of Wales, this traditional Welsh farmhouse is built entirely of slate. The walls are thick slate slabs bonded together with lime mortar, while on top is a classic slate roof. Notice the decorative arched slate lintel above the front door.

Internal use

Easily identifiable because of its grey colour, slate is suitable for external and internal uses. Here, recalling traditional stone wall construction, slate creates a striking surround for a contemporary fireplace. Slabs of different sizes are interlocked to build the decorative wall.

Tile (covering)

Whereas slate is a naturally occurring material, which is simply shaped for use, tiles are manufactured from a variety of materials including ceramic, stone, glass or even metal. While the latter two are less common, ceramic and stoneware tiles have been a mainstay in construction for many years – particularly the red/brown ceramic and terracotta (Italian for 'baked earth') tiles. These are formed into the desired shape, often with a curved 'S' profile so that they can be laid on a roof and interlocked to form a good waterproof covering. Along the roof ridge and down the gables half-round tiles are laid and cemented in place to cover the gap where the edges of the tile courses meet. Today, tiles of similar style are also manufactured from concrete.

Catalan flourish

Designed by Antoni Gaudí for the industrialist Manuel Vicens, Casa Vicens is an amazing tile-clad house in Barcelona, Spain. Built of brick, the house is covered with thousands of the ceramic tiles manufactured by Vicens at his brick and tile factory. The architectural flourishes and chequerboard designs reveal Gaudí's Moorish influence at the time.

Polychrome roof (left)

Far from being a mere waterproof roof covering, tiles can and, for many years, have been used to decorative effect. Fired stoneware tiles can be coloured during the manufacturing process and distinctive designs such as this, typical of grander dwellings in Burgundy, France, show just what is possible.

Complete tile façade

Eric Westerneng's home/office in Purmerend, The Netherlands, is partially clad in high-gloss, glazed clay roof tiles. The same tiles are used on the main house roof and on the circular walls of the office, too. They are fixed to wooden laths via stainless steel screws and tile hooks.

Decorative wall tiling

It may look like wallpaper but the external wall of this Portuguese house is covered in ceramic tiles. Both decorative and hardwearing, the tiles are weatherproof and fun to look at. While few houses are finished in this way today, tiled façades were common in the late 19th and early 20th centuries.

Wood (covering)

Scribe's shingles
Naulakha, Rudyard
Kipling's Vermont home,
is a classic example
of a US shingle-style
house. Built on a stone
foundation, the timber
frame is clad almost
entirely in wooden
shingles. This covering
sheds water in the same
way as fired earthenware
tiles, while gracefully
ageing with the building,
slowly changing colour
over time.

There are many types of timber façade for the house, from structural solutions, such as the log cabin, to weatherproof board finishes or permeable rain screens. Some are intentionally porous to allow cooling breezes to circulate in summer. Others are completely water and air tight to ensure effective insulation and energy conservation. Wood is considered a good option because, if sourced responsibly, it is environmentally friendly (the forest can be managed, and growing trees capture carbon from the atmosphere). Whatever the location or design requirement, wood has probably been tried at some point, and most probably found to be a good material to use.

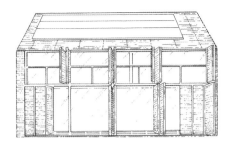

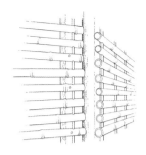

Bamboo building (above)

Technically a grass rather than wood, bamboo is an interesting and highly sustainable material for construction. This house in France is clad in a see-through skin of bamboo (*see above detail*), which creates a partial weather screen and great shading for the interior. The bamboo is fixed on steel cables within metal frames.

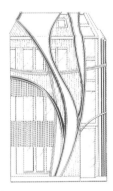

Board and batten façade

The board and batten façade is an inexpensive and easy to install solution to cladding the exterior of many a house (mine included). Wide timber boards are fixed vertically onto the building's timber frame and then thinner battens are added to cover the butted joints of the wide boards. The façade is fully waterproofed with a coat of paint or stain.

Artistic solution

Celebrating the vibrancy and warmth of wood, along with its ease of workability, 24H Architects designed this house in The Netherlands. The façade is a combination of timber and rusted metal. Those prominent curved timber ribs could be interpreted as reminders of where the material used to make the façade came from.

Glass

Clearly curvaceous
Lake Lugano House in
Switzerland, by Italian
practice JM Architecture,
uses glass for contrast in
this house on two levels.
The lower level has
more conventional solid
walls with windows but
the upper living area is
a beautiful fully glazed
pavilion with curved
corners that add to the
luxurious feel of the
house. Highly efficient,
low-emittance glass
insulated with argon gas
optimises the thermal
efficiency of the shell.

What did we do before glass? Windows were holes in
the wall, which may or may not have been covered by
animal hide, wooden shutters or similar before glazing
became affordable. Flattened animal horn made a
translucent covering around the 14th century, but it
wasn't until the 17th century that glass became widely
used. Today, entire buildings are built of glass. It can
be crystal clear, coloured, textured, opaque or solar-
reflective. Glass is a vital part of almost all houses and
the way it is used often indicates the style of house,
too. Small leaded window panes suggest an historic
bent, while expansive sheets of clear glazing lean more
towards the Modernist ideals. Glass is an integral part
of our home both functionally and as part of the style
and ambiance of the house.

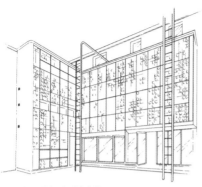

Modern ideals (right)

Clad almost entirely in glass, a modern Romanian house, by WigWam Design, uses the material as the wall infill to the rolled steel beam framework. This is Modernist architecture taken to its logical end – the materials used are few, the design is clever in its simplicity, and the glass accentuates the minimalistic nature of the entire building.

Glass bricks (left)

Built entirely of glass brick, Maison de Verre (house of glass) in Paris, France, was a collaboration between a designer, Pierre Chareau, and an architect, Bernard Bijvoet, in the late 1920s. The design uses industrial materials, including glass bricks. Here the bricks, being structural, are laid as conventional bricks would be – with a mortar joint.

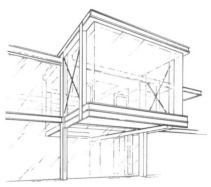

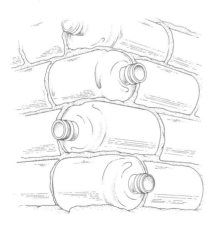

Recycled glass

Glass comes in many forms, and, long before flat panes were manufactured for windows, craftsmen were making bottles and other glass vessels to put things in. Therefore, it seems fitting to use such bottles to build a house. Here glass bottles are used like bricks to build the walls: the air inside creates an insulative barrier, so keeping the home warm.

Metal (covering)

Metal is widely used in construction as a structural medium, around which houses are constructed. However, there are other applications for its use, for example as an exterior weatherproof covering. Whether in impermeable sheet form, or as the external element of a breathable façade, such as a rain screen, metal of one kind or another has been used to clad houses. When treated it is long lasting, and metals such as copper weather with time to provide beautiful finishes that evolve with the age of the house. From an economical pressed-steel siding to the expensive CorTen steel that architects like to use, metal offers diverse options for the designer and house builder of the 21st century.

Metal magic

40_R Laneway House in Toronto, Canada, by architect Superkül is an example of how metal can be used to clad a house. The design turns an existing building into a unique architectural statement that echoes its industrial past. The principle behind the use of metal as a covering would be the same for any house. The rust colour is the finish of the material (here CorTen steel). It will remain like that for the life of the building.

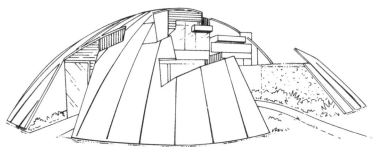

Traditional standing seam roof (above)

The standing seam roof, named on account of the metal ridges that are formed as rolled joints at the edge of the sheets, has long been used as a domestic and industrial roof covering. Here, it crowns a colonial-style house in Parramatta, a suburb of Sydney, Australia. The roof material can be tin, steel or even lead.

Metal in disguise

Shaped like tiles, and the colour of tiles, a roof can be constructed from metal sheets pressed into a form resembling the more traditional but labour-intensive tiled roof.

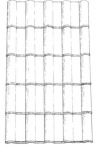

Ribbed copper façade

The shape and design of this domed house may well be unusual but the external façade is a simple, yet striking, covering of copper sheets. Copper is often used on the exterior of buildings, either in its raw, polished form, or in its green coloured (or 'patinated') form, in which style it can either be manufactured or allowed to weather into over time.

Render (covering)

Stucco chic

This painted mansion in Tucson, Arizona, Owls Club Mansion, is a prime example of a Mission Revival style house that has been finished in stucco. Notice how the stucco has been used not only to coat the exterior but also to decorate the central balcony and pilasters. Skilled artisans can create all manner of decorative effects with stucco and conventional cement-based render.

The tradition of applying a covering of a wet mud-based material to the exterior of a house, which will then dry into a hard weatherproof outer skin, is millennia old. Stucco is an ancient method, using lime, sand and water. However, today the more common materials are cement, sand and water. Both types of render mix produce a smooth paste-like material, which can be applied easily to any rough, porous surface with a trowel. Certain parts of the world are renowned for their rendered buildings. The islands of Greece and other Mediterranean places abound with white-painted, rendered buildings, while in the southern states of America and Mexico stucco is a traditional finish to buildings both old and new.

Wattle and daub

Wattle and daub is an ancient construction technique, from which many newer ones were developed. Used to fill in sections of wall between large structural timbers, the technique involves weaving semi-rigid mats of reed or wood and fixing them into the wall. Then a mix of mud, animal dung and grass is applied to the mats, bonding to their textured surface. After drying, the wall becomes strong and hard.

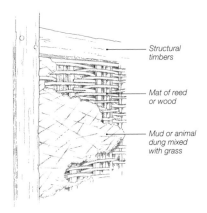

Structural timbers

Mat of reed or wood

Mud or animal dung mixed with grass

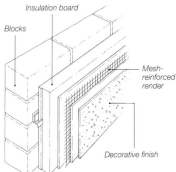

Insulation board

Blocks

Mesh-reinforced render

Decorative finish

Modern rendered wall

Today, a rendered wall is far more than mud and grass. This wall system is constructed from multiple layers including a rigid insulation board, mesh-reinforced render and a thin decorative finish. This type of construction is common on newer homes in mass-housing schemes.

Decorative effects

Render and stucco have the added benefit of being pliable while wet and traditionally craftsfolk made good use of this. Pargeting, as the technique is called, involves either sculpting raised patterns or scraping or stamping recessed patterns into wet render. This decorative effect was common during the 15th and 16th centuries in England and Europe; thereafter the Spanish introduced it to the Americas.

Introduction

Georgian grace
Georgian architecture is perhaps one of the most straightforward styles: houses tended to be designed with symmetry and restraint in mind. Hammond-Harwood House, in Annapolis, Maryland, has a main volume crowned with a large pediment. On either side are identical wings. Low-pitched, hipped roofs and simple sash windows add to the sense of demure elegance.

What makes a building a house? This question is easier to answer than: What makes a house a home? because everyone has a different take on that. A house, whether located in America or Armenia, New Zealand or The Netherlands, has, with a few very unusual exceptions, the same set of constituent parts. From the ground up, there are foundations, a floor slab, walls and a roof. Then you have the necessary accoutrements, such as doors, windows, internal walls and staircases. Finally there are the finishes and flourishes that some may consider turn that house into a home: the inviting porch or veranda, perhaps a balcony or other external appendage, plus internal decorations including cornices, mouldings, columns and pilasters.

Neoclassical excess
While Georgian architecture focused on form, Neoclassical designs explode with extravagant decoration. Graceland, the onetime home of Elvis Presley in Memphis, Tennessee, is adorned with rusticated walls, a huge white portico, windows (both arched and not), plus chimney stacks with stone cornices. Each part is grander than the next, and every part has decoration of some sort.

Every home has its basic built requirements and then the special features that turn it from what Modernists refer to as a 'machine for living' into a style of house suited to one person, if not another.

While the aforementioned features and flourishes tend to alert house-style sleuths to the influences of the designer or builder of the house, clues can also be garnered from the type of construction of the building. These can be clues to the style, or they can be indicative of the location in which the house is built – a house that is built on stilts may well be built on a floodplain or subject to monsoon rains. This type of construction would be deemed redundant if used in an English village, but transpose that house to parts of India and it becomes a necessary design trait.

The parts that define a house can take on a different appearance depending upon style and location. However, together they form what we know as a place to live and this chapter examines the differences and similarities between them.

Foundations

The foundation is the base upon which the house is built. There are many different types, from historic stone corbels stacked into shallow trenches to highly designed rafts of prestressed concrete beams that float as a single entity above ground prone to move and heave in an uneven manner. No matter what type of foundation a house sits on, its role is to provide a stable base from which to build upwards. Today, architects and engineers go to great lengths to analyse the ground conditions before designing a foundation. Historically, trial and error prevailed and eventually a stable, easily buildable type of foundation was developed. For obvious reasons, foundations are not a stylistic element of house design. They are more often than not forgotten about, until they fail, when the results can be catastrophic.

Traditional stone/rubble
Stacked in a trench, which is then backfilled, large stones make for a strong foundation. They may or may not be bonded together with a lime mortar but most important is setting the stones in place well, leaving as few gaps and chance for structural failure as possible. Stone foundations were common until fired earth bricks became widely used.

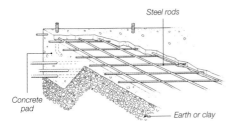

Steel rods

Concrete pad

Earth or clay

Raft

Thicker at its extremities (where the external walls will be) than across the middle portion, a raft foundation is a thick concrete pad on which the house will be built. Reinforced with steel rods the raft is designed to float on ground such as clay, which would crack conventional trench foundations as it heaves and sinks.

Post

A very simple foundation, often used in areas where houses are lifted off the ground to alleviate flooding damage, the post foundation is a series of holes partially filled with concrete or crushed rock. The structural frame of the house sits on this pad and the hole is filled in, around the post, to ground level.

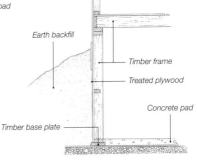

Concrete pad

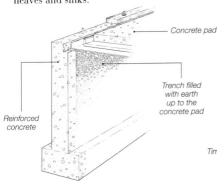

Concrete pad

Trench filled with earth up to the concrete pad

Reinforced concrete

Earth backfill

Timber frame

Treated plywood

Concrete pad

Timber base plate

Conventional footing

The footing, the most common of all foundations, is a reinforced concrete pad. Liquid concrete is poured into the bottom of a trench dug in the earth in the pattern of the house's load-bearing walls. Brick or blocks are built up from the concrete pad and then the trench is filled in around them to ground level.

Treated wood

Wood can be used in foundations once it has been pretreated to resist moisture ingress. Here, a timber frame clad in treated plywood rests on a timber base plate. The trench that it is in has been backfilled with earth and the relatively light timber frame of the house is quickly built up above ground level.

COMPONENTS **Walls**

Brick cavity

Extremely common in the UK and northern Europe, the cavity wall is built of two skins of bricks or blocks, laid in interlocking courses. The two parallel walls are tied together with metal straps called cavity ties. The gap between the walls prevents water penetrating from the exterior to the interior and also acts as an insulator (it may be filled with insulating material).

The wall may appear obvious; it is the bit that holds up the roof and keeps the weather out. But walls come in many different types. They are made of different materials; left exposed or clad in a variety of finishes; built to be rigid or flexible, strong or light; or all of the aforementioned and more. Historically, it was easy to gauge what a wall was made of because you could see it: from the Tudor timber frame with wattle and daub infill to the brick wall that is so prevalent in the UK and northern Europe. But elsewhere the structural elements of many walls are hidden by an outer coating of wet or dry finish materials, such as stucco plaster or timber cladding. Walls *are* the part that holds the roof up, but they also provide great clues to a house's architectural origins.

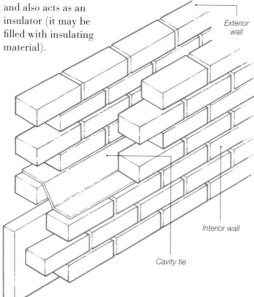

Exterior wall

Interior wall

Cavity tie

Traditional log cabin

One of the simplest of all walls is that used to build traditional log cabins. Tree trunks, felled, stripped of branches and peeled of their bark, are laid in the shape of the building. Each ascending layer of logs is interlocked at the corners to create a rigid outer wall. Gaps between the logs are often plugged with moss, ferns or grasses, held in place by clay.

Modern log cabin

An engineered version of the log wall is now widely available. Constructed from machined timbers which interlock, the wall has a cavity – much like its brick cousin – that is filled with insulation. Instead of notching the timbers at their corners, bolts are used to pin them together, creating a strong wall that will stand up well to the rigours of 21st-century living.

Modern rainscreen

Many modern house and office walls are covered in rainscreen cladding. The outer covering, which can be natural or manmade, keeps rain off the interior elements but is not weathertight. Instead, a gap behind it allows air to flow, so draining moisture from within the wall. Behind the waterproof membrane are the main structure, insulation and inner wall covering.

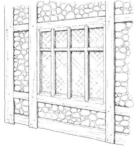

Tudor panelled

Heavy timbers, sometimes 15–20 cm (6–8 in) across, were used as the main structural members of many Tudor houses. Between this framework was an infill called 'wattle and daub', which consisted of either sticks or stones over which was plastered a mix of mud and lime that set to provide a hard, weatherproof wall.

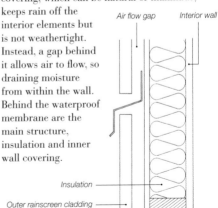

Air flow gap Interior wall

Insulation

Outer rainscreen cladding

Floors

Suspended timber
Supported on the external wall of the house, plus a brick pier built off a concrete pad, a suspended floor has wooden joists as its main structural frame, onto which a subfloor covering of plywood boards is laid. Finally, the top covering is laid over the boards, which may be polished wood floorboards, a carpet or tiles.

Floors come in many forms, although almost all are flat! From ancient times people have modified the internal floor of their homes, whether by scraping a clean area of earth or insetting stones or other materials, to decorate or elevate the floor in some way. As buildings became more sophisticated so did the floors within them. Initially, the addition of a second storey, along with its suspended floor, was a triumph but soon multiple storeys and ever more elaborate methods of supporting them became common. Today, floors are made of many materials and designed to do everything from cushion the tread of occupants to heat the room they are laid within.

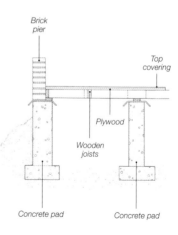

Brick pier

Top covering

Plywood

Wooden joists

Concrete pad

Concrete pad

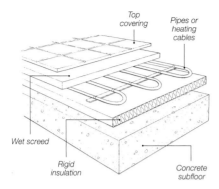

Top covering

Pipes or heating cables

Wet screed

Rigid insulation

Concrete subfloor

Modern heated floor

One of the most modern flooring innovations is the heated floor. Here, a poured concrete subfloor is overlaid with rigid insulation. On top of this a network of pipes or electrical heating cables is installed (if pipes are used they carry hot water). A wet screed is laid over them and finally a top covering is put down.

Precast concrete floor

For speed of construction, the precast concrete floor is hard to beat. Large prestressed, reinforced concrete beams are lifted into position by a crane and placed side by side. Once the beams are installed, a subfloor covering of screed or concrete is laid, before the final cover is put down.

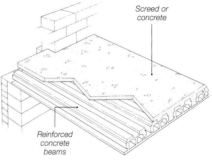

Screed or concrete

Reinforced concrete beams

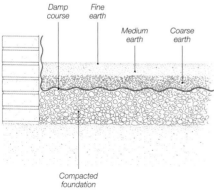

Damp course

Fine earth

Medium earth

Coarse earth

Compacted foundation

Earth floor

Earth floors may sound simple to install but if they are to last, the correct materials have to be used, and they must be compacted well so as not to quickly break up. Two methods of earth floor construction feature graduated layers consisting of a compacted foundation, followed by either a top covering of packed earth or cobbled stones.

Roofs

Timeless terracotta
Manufactured as long ago as in ancient Greece, clay tiles come in many shapes and sizes but they all perform the same weatherproofing job. Here, so-called barrel tiles – semi-circular in form – are laid in tight convex-concave-convex formation to form hills and channels to drain water off the roof of an old building.

The roof is the crowning glory of a building, and a part of it that is most often used to make a statement. Each differing style and period of architecture tends to have a specific roof design, or at least a favoured pitch. Take Gothic architecture as an example: its steeply pitched roofs, spires and towers can turn relatively sedate buildings into dramatic houses, churches or cathedrals. In contrast, the shallow pitch and lack of decoration associated with Georgian roof design only strengthens the genre's image as a restrained style. But, style aside, the roof must also shelter the building it covers from the weather. Whether flat or steeply pitched, and with or without dormers or spires, no roof is a good roof unless it can do this.

Gothic tower

Like a witch's hat, perched atop a
cylindrical tower this Gothic-inspired detail
is a fitting crown on a Victorian-style house.
Such an extravagant flourish is common on
houses of the era in America but less so in
other parts of the world where Victorian
design was somewhat less flamboyant.

Victorian gable and porch

Almost emblematic, the Victorian gable
is an easy clue for any budding house-
style sleuth. A pitch of 45 degrees or more
is normal, while detailing to both gable
and porch (shown in the bargeboards)
is a flourish that was often taken to the
extremes by the designers of yesteryear.

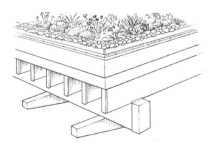

Growing flat roof

Although there are old examples
of grass-covered roofs, the practice
of designing a roof that will encourage
vegetation growth on it is now becoming
more common on new buildings. The
reasons for it are added insulation,
water retention (lessening the impact
upon sewer systems) and encouraging
biodiversity in urban neighbourhoods.

Windows & Doors

First impressions

Doors and windows can be more than points of access, or a way of filling interiors with light and air. Their number, arrangement and scale can also be a statement, both of the architect's appreciation of symmetry and grandeur, and of the harmonious use of local materials and skills that imbue a sense of place.

While windows and doors are essential elements of a building's weatherproofing, they are also components that can be manipulated to suit a style. Both features have been changed throughout architectural history to suit tastes: their size, shape and decorative aspects being moulded to take on Renaissance, Prairie, Modern and any number of other traits. Along with the roof, the doors and windows are a good place to start when trying to work out the style of a house. Look for arches (and their particular shape); different types of opening mechanism; size of window pane and overall number, size and shape of the openings in the building's façade.

Gothic

Even on a relatively small one-and-a-half-storey cottage, the doorway and dormer window above make for a dramatic spectacle. In this case, the pointed arch of both door and window, plus the steep roof on the dormer and its pinnacle, tell us that the design is Gothic-inspired.

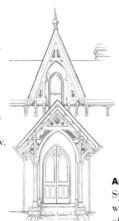

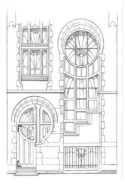

Art Nouveau

Symmetrical architectural elements coupled with unusual design traits, such as this pair of single doors set within a single arch, challenge the house-style hunter. However, the wonderful sloped panelling and curved triple lights on each door mark this design out as Art Nouveau, a style as much associated with art as architecture.

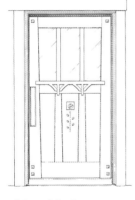

Arts and Crafts

Arts and Crafts design encompasses many techniques but the defining principle is that it has been made by hand – that is, crafted. This beautiful front door has tapered jambs, wrought-iron bolts and latch set, plus wooden decorative touches that mark it out from mass-produced products.

Modernist

Modernism shuns decoration and could therefore be thought of as bland. However, the unusual design and shape of windows, such as these differently sized ribbon ones, and the minimal design of the window frames can serve to add intrigue to houses that would otherwise be large and boxy.

Staircases

While roofs, doors and windows offer chances to elaborate on an architectural style on the exterior of a building, one of the primary internal features of many houses, and therefore a place to create drama, is the staircase. Fancy wooden newel posts and balusters are a mainstay of Victorian design; sweeping double staircases that descend into double-height reception spaces were the thing for Renaissance and Neoclassical architects; while minimising the stair to its bare skeleton and even removing the stringer are approaches that Modernist-inspired architects still favour today. Whatever the style, there is a staircase design indicative of it. Whatever the material – from wood to steel and even glass – there is a staircase built out of it, such is the architects' predilection for using them as signals of style.

Art Nouveau

The steps curve gracefully as they descend to the base of this Art Nouveau stairwell. The sweep of the handrail and its extravagantly scrolled design completes a wonderfully artistic piece of design. Such curves and flourishes are indicative of an architectural style, which grew out of the arts movement of the same name.

Arts and Crafts

Extolling the virtues of malleable materials, such as wood, was one of the main interests of Arts and Crafts designers and makers. This staircase and surround use a variety of joints and cutting techniques to build a structure that is robust while at the same time being pleasing to the eye.

Renaissance (left)

Multiple half landings, extravagantly turned balusters and newel posts, plus the semicircular (bull-nosed) curve of the bottom step allude to the Renaissance-inspired design of this staircase. These elements are all gleaned from much grander staircases in the châteaux and villas of France and Italy.

Minimalist

Stripping the staircase back to its most basic, and then painting it white to blend into the wall supporting it, is a trait often used by Modernist and Minimalist designers. Here, the reinforced concrete stair is devoid of handrail or protective tread coverings; it is as the staircases of many modern houses would be before they are covered in wood or carpet.

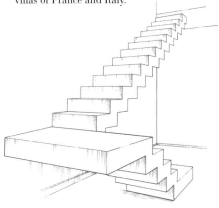

Balconies & Porches

Modernist veranda

Modernist architects, such as the designer of this house, Mies van der Rohe, would call this veranda an 'outside room', which is what it is; an extension of the overall house, albeit without walls. It is a common trait of Modernist houses where decorative additions such as balconies are eschewed but people are still able to enjoy a shaded outdoor space.

Similar to fire surrounds and gallery landings in the interiors of houses, balconies and porches are external decorative additions which are very often not strictly necessary in terms of making the building complete, but are used very frequently by architects and builders who want to add interest to a relatively blank façade. Having said that, large structure-like wrap-around verandas and *portes cochères* can protect users from the sun and rain to some extent. However, the ornate styling of small balconies and ornamental porches far outweighs their practical use. Look out for size and location, followed by baluster design or pediment detailing, for clues about the style of a porch or balcony.

Tudor balcony

This balcony was designed more for practical use than as a decorative flourish. The simple wooden handrail and square section balusters echo the timber framing of the building itself. You can imagine the occupants going out onto the balcony to empty the contents of their chamber pot into the street below.

Colonial-style wraparound veranda

John Griswold House, in Newport, Rhode Island, is adorned with a veranda sweeping around two elevations of the building. The veranda is supported on Classical Greek style columns, but two different types of handrail to the steps confuse the overall architectural aesthetic.

Georgian porch

Apart from its two Greek-inspired Ionic columns, this porch is proportioned and restrained in the Georgian style. The round columns are interesting though: scrolled tops mark them as Ionic but plain shafts hint also at Doric or Tuscan influence.

Prairie-style balcony

Frank Lloyd Wright designed this house with no fewer than three balconies that run the entire length of the façades to which they are attached. White stone capping further elongates their form and adds to the building's overall linearity.

Decorations

While thus far elements such as doors, windows, balconies, porches and roofs have all been described in relation to their decorative aspects and the artistic interest they add to a basic building, there are some things that, while important, are nonetheless just there for decoration. The shape of a column capital, the intricacy of gingerbread tracery, forms of balusters, pointy pinnacles, all are added to the design of a house because the architect believes that they contribute to the style and appeal of the building. This is true unless you are a fan of Modernism, in which case the simple act of stripping all decoration to its minimum is the way to go.

Pattern making

Ever since the ancient Greeks fluted their columns, patterns have been part of the architect's armoury. Friezes carved into the centre of pediments adorning grand temples, or pilasters (such as this one here) running down the side of windows on residential Victorian houses, all add to the design drama and overall appeal of the different architectural genres.

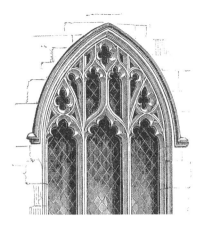

Gothic tracery

The pointed arch at the head of this window is one indication that it is Gothic in style. The other is the beautifully carved stone tracery within the window frame. Its form and intricacy is something often seen in Gothic cathedrals and sometimes spotted in the window of the gatehouse to a grand house or a parson's churchside abode.

Arts and Crafts panel

Wood carving has been employed as decoration for almost as long as people have been building houses, but the Arts and Crafts movement probably took it to heart more than any other. Here a decorative chimney piece is adorned with oak trees and shields. The wooden element clad the exterior of a brick or stone fireplace.

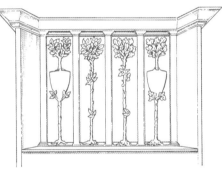

Renaissance detail

The cornice, which runs around the roof eaves of a building's exterior or the ceiling edge of its interior, is a decorative effect that has been employed by many architectural movements, from Victorian to Modern-eclectic. Renaissance architects had a great affection for cornices such as the intricately decorated one, seen here, on the Palazzo Farnese in Rome.

House Styles

Equipped with the vocabulary of house types, materials and components, the chapters in the following section will help you to put that knowledge of domestic architecture into practice by identifying the key architectural styles and movements, beginning with the Tudor period.

Of course, many houses do not fit into a single style category, as subsequent additions and renovations disguise if not completely obliterate their origin and architectural history. There are, though, always visual clues to collect and connect to particular design trends – historic or contemporary. For example, developers

often built houses to a template, which, once recognised, is easy to spot whatever the context. However, craftsman homes are more typically individual, one-off designs, built more for love than money: even so, they have traits and trends that mark them out from houses of other eras. Learning to identify the key architectural styles and their characteristic features allows you to piece together the history of different houses, great and small, and to readily distinguish between Mock Tudor and Modernist, Renaissance and Classical Revival, Pueblo and Prairie or kit and kitsch. Good luck.

TUDOR Introduction

The Tudors ruled England from 1485 to 1603. The architectural style developed during this period lifted domestic design out of medieval times, introducing houses which could be regarded as relatively 'normal' by today's standards.

Houses of this period are characterised by black timbers and white infill panels. This distinctive style was not dreamed up by designers but an honest way of building with materials close to hand. With much of England forested, wood was easy to come by and the infill panels were constructed of wattle and daub – mud and sticks – making them inexpensive to create. Some more elaborate buildings also featured brick infill panels, often in a herringbone pattern. The Tudor House Museum in Southampton demonstrates some typical Tudor traits, for example the upper floors extend beyond the first floor and the windows and doorways are topped with flat arches. The relatively simple nature of the façade is beautifully contrasted against internal features such as the wood-panelled ceilings, which are wonderfully crafted. It is a great place to visit to get to understand how houses this old were built.

Tudor House Museum
Built in the late 15th century, this wealthy trader's home changed hands frequently over the next 200 years before falling into disrepair in the late 18th century. Today, it is a museum, restored as a fine example of Tudor house design.

True Tudor houses can only be those built in the 15th and 16th centuries; Tudor Revival or 'Mock Tudor' architecture emerged in the late 19th century and persists to the present day. It celebrates the main aesthetic elements of Tudor architecture, while combining them with more up to date construction methods.

One of the defining traits of a Tudor Revival house is the dark timbers with infill panels. More often than not these timbers no longer bear any structural weight: instead they are stuck on to the house walls as part of the decoration. Between them a stucco plaster is added and painted white.

However, not all Tudor Revival houses are so obvious. Steeply pitched roofs are a good clue, as are the arches that can be seen within the façade finish and above the windows. Most important, however, is the chimney breast. The Tudors flaunted the fact that a house had an enclosed fireplace, an innovation in the 15th century. This is what makes tapping into the design ideal of a house so interesting – as we begin to understand why the architect of such a house decided to make the chimney stack so prominent, we begin to appreciate the nuances of both the original architectural tradition and the later emulation of that tradition.

Presidential revival
Designed and built for Woodrow Wilson, 28th president of the United States, this house in Princeton, New Jersey, was not completed until late in the 19th century. Its style, however, is very Tudor. Known as Tudor Revival, these houses accentuate aspects such as the black timber beams and whitewashed walls of their 15th- and 16th-century forebears but with a geometric perfection that could not be achieved in years gone by.

TUDOR Archetypes

Detail in design

Manoir de Coupesarte, in the Auge village of Coupesarte, northwest France, is a wonderful example of the exquisite detailing that some Tudor houses display. Here, the timber framing is used as a decorative medium as well as a structural element, and bricks are used as infill, a distinct contrast to the black and white Tudor norm.

Houses of the Tudor period take on a different look depending upon where they were built. Here, a 15th-century French manor house is markedly different from properties of the same period in, say, the capital, Paris. Built as a private dwelling and surrounded on three sides by water, the Manoir de Coupesarte is one of an astonishing number of well-preserved half-timbered farm and manor houses that dot the Auge countryside in rural Normandy. Part of its charm lies in its irregular design, the uneven framework of beams (known as *colombages*) infilled with red brick and the two slate-tiled turrets that project over the water.

Fifteenth-century vernacular design

Lack of symmetry, an overhanging second storey and steeply pitched roof are Tudor hallmarks. The main difference in this house in St Sulpice de Grimbouville, Eure is the thatched roof, a reflection of the abundance of straw or reeds in northern France. The eaves' deep overhang requires support in the form of timber brackets or corbels.

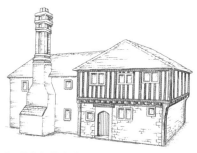

English half-timbered

This English house is a classic example of Tudor architecture. Partially built of brick, with a black and white timbered upper storey, which overhangs the first floor, the house features a large and decorative chimney stack. Windows appear almost random in their positioning and size.

American Tudor Revival

This Minneapolis house, built in the late 1890s, forgoes decorative timbers and concentrates on the architectural form of the Tudor period, with steeply pitched roofs and arches above the windows. Note the positioning of the chimney breast, recalling the Tudor desire to flaunt the fact that the house had an enclosed fireplace.

Twentieth-century Tudor

Pinner House was not built until the early 20th century, and its location is Dunedin, New Zealand, but it is a prime example of Tudor design. Dubbed Tudor Revival or mock Tudor, the style focuses primarily on half-timbered façades with stucco finish infill panels. Renowned architect Francis Petre designed this building.

TUDOR Archetypes

A bishop's house?

The property on which Bishops House is built is thought to have been owned by John de Blithe and his descendants. Two of the family were bishops but there is no evidence that either of them lived in the house. However, the name has stuck and any lack of bishops does not take away from the house's beautiful Tudor design.

While Tudor style changed over time, this is perhaps the iconic ideal of a property from the period. Typical of a large farm or manorhouse from the 15th century, Bishops House in Sheffield, has the unmistakable features of a Tudor house. Although its roof is not as steeply pitched as other houses of the period, the use of both stone and the black and white upper storey is clearly Tudor. Internally the rooms feature deeply coffered ceilings, the heavy beams used to support the upper storey running both ways and being painted white to lessen their visual impact on the relatively low-ceilinged dwelling.

Swiss style

Taking the basic Tudor ideal and adding local design flair, this Swiss house in Lucerne is an example of how a style can be manipulated by architects or master builders in different parts of the world. Cross braces to the panels have been elaborately carved to decorative effect.

Twin Tudors (right)

While it looks like two adjoining properties, this building is actually one house and was formerly the home of the Herbert family. Located in York, England, it has withstood the ravages of time, even if the long heavy beams that run across its width may have sagged a little.

New Tudor

Even today architects are designing houses that include a nod to the Tudor period. This house in Minnesota, USA, is an eclectic mix of Ranch style (note the low-pitched roof) and Tudor: the timber- and plaster-finished upper storey revealing the Tudor aspect. While the design is rather muddled, the influence of Tudor architecture is obvious for all to see.

TUDOR

Queen Elizabeth's Hunting Lodge, 1543

The Great Standing

Imagine this building with the walls of its uppermost floor open apart from the timber frame. This is how it would have looked when originally built: the reason, to allow guests to take pot shots at game, while being entertained by the king. The walls were later filled in to make it more comfortable to live in.

Not a palace by any means but still a royal abode, Queen Elizabeth's Hunting Lodge in Chingford, Essex, was originally built for King Henry VIII and called 'the Great Standing', but the house was also used by his daughter Queen Elizabeth after his death. Henry and his guests would have surveyed the hunt from its upper floors and shot at deer as they were herded past. Glazed windows were not installed until after 1650. The lodge is unusual in that its structural timber frame is painted white to match the wattle and daub infill panels, thus marking it out from the black and white Tudor houses of the time. Inside, the building has been fully restored and now acts as a museum, housing a display of Tudor artefacts and crafts, including carpentry and examples of the wooden joints used by craftsmen of the day.

Chimney stack

Although relatively devoid of ornamentation, the chimney stack is a prominent feature of the building. This is in part because enclosed fireplaces and chimney flues were a new invention, and also because it is safer to place the hot fire flue on the outside of the building, as opposed to encasing it within the timber structure.

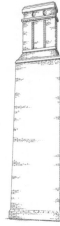

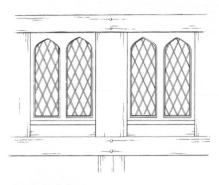

Leaded windows

The glazed windows in Queen Elizabeth's Hunting Lodge were not installed until 1650, a century after its construction. Originally, Henry VIII and guests would have used the openings to shoot through. However, the small leaded window lights are in keeping with Tudor style and their addition does nothing to detract from the house's quirky grandeur.

Timbered external façade

Even though the timbers on the house's façade have been painted white they are still plainly visible. They form square and rectangular panels which are cross braced by diagonal timbers to stop the structure from 'racking' (collapsing sideways on itself in high winds).

Internal timber framing

The interior of the building is similar to the exterior, apart from the fact that the wooden structural timbers have not been painted white. Inside they remain black and add a touch of elegance to the large space at the top of the house that was once the main shooting terrace and banqueting hall.

Materials & Construction

A different Tudor
Kahn's use of stone echoes the houses of the Cotswolds, which are also stone-built. The result is a less recognisable style of Tudor house, which has to be studied for form and features to be comprehended. Stone, however, was used in Tudor times, although this house was built in Tudoresque style at a much later date.

Gaukler Point, designed by pre-eminent American architect Albert Kahn for Edsel and Eleanor Ford, is a marvellous example of a designer taking reference from an historical style in order to create a new home. Gaukler Point, sited on the shore of Lake St Clair northeast of Detroit, Michigan, was not built until 1926 but Kahn designed it in the Tudoresque style of houses in the English Cotswolds. However, being 400 years younger than the houses it is inspired by, the Fords' house is able to incorporate larger windows, cast chimney pots and lead flashings to the hips and lean-to elements of the roof.

Upward and outward

The upper storeys of many Tudor houses extend out further than the lower ones. This extension is enabled by large beams that protrude beyond the wall of the lower storey. Some houses also feature wooden support brackets called corbels, although these often serve a decorative rather than structural purpose.

Framed wonders

Half-timbering, or even full-timbering, is a technique that used a framework of large wooden beams and columns to build the walls of a house. Between this frame are infill panels of bricks or wooden sticks coated in mud and lime – known as wattle and daub.

Making a statement

The large chimney breasts and tall, often ornate chimneys that can be seen on Tudor houses were a status symbol of the day. These features proclaimed that the house had an enclosed fireplace, an innovation that allowed for two storeys because it funnelled smoke from the main living space out of the building.

Doors & Windows

Tudor additions

Ascott House, near Wing in Buckinghamshire, has been added to again and again over a period of three hundred years. However, all new extensions to the property have been in keeping with the original style and the house loses none of its period charm for these newer elements.

Originally a farmhouse built in 1606, Ascott House has since undergone many changes. Architect George Devey was employed by Leopold de Rothschild in the 1800s to expand the house to create a hunting lodge and country house. Devey's additions were true to the original Tudor design – even though windows could be made without leaded lights, the architect insisted on designing traditional small Tudor windows with diagonal criss-cross leaded panes. The entrance is also interesting, featuring a porch with a Tudor-style flat arch opening, rather than the later pointed Gothic or semicircular Roman arch. It also boasts a canopy, somewhat out of character with the rest of the house.

Small-paned windows

Sutton House in Hackney, east London, has classical Tudor windows. Glass making was in its relative infancy and so only small pieces of clear glazing could be made. The solution was to manufacture windows made of many small pieces of glass joined together with strips of lead.

Steep-pitched porch

Porches most often reflect the style of roof employed on a property. Tudor porches predominantly feature steeply pitched roofs to match the house roof. They can be covered in slate, tile or thatch, depending upon the material most easily available in the vicinity of the house.

Extended windows

Many Tudor properties, and those before them, suffered from being quite dark inside. This was the result of a window tax (paid on the number of windows in a house). Master builders came up with a solution: extended bay-type windows, which joined together multiple panes to create a large glazed window opening.

Multiple-panelled door

Doors on Tudor houses are multiple panelled because craftsmen manufactured them from wood before such modern innovations as particle board and plywood were invented. The use of smaller sections of timber meant that doors had to be pieced together using planks of a frame and panels.

TUDOR Ornamentation

Reserved grandeur
Built in 1888 by philanthropist William Hesketh Lever for workers at his Sunlight soap factory on the Wirral in northwest England, the Port Sunlight Houses are a fine example of Tudor Revival architecture. They were built more than two centuries after Tudor first came to the fore, yet they retain the classic black and white styling, making them instantly recognisable.

Overt expressions of ornamentation were not something that the designers of Tudor buildings dwelt upon, often because the construction of extrovert ornamental additions was costly and extremely difficult to achieve using relatively primitive materials and techniques. However, what they lacked in fanciful balconies, turrets and pinnacles, Tudor houses made up for in strength of design and robust beauty. Houses big and small were, and still are, easily identifiable because of the common use of black and white timbers and infill panels. While this construction type was entirely functional – a structural timber frame and weatherproof panels filling the gaps – it also created a visually striking style that is still mimicked today.

Decorative cornice

Decorative detailing was often subdued on Tudor houses but the wooden cornice at roof level and often between floors was a chance for craftsmen to show off their skills. Designs varied from simple repetitive patterns to floral and animal forms that can be quite intricate.

Ornate chimneys

Boasting the fact that a house contained an enclosed fireplace, brick chimneys would feature swirling designs or intricate changes in brick bond, making them the theatrical crown of many a Tudor house.

Decorative half-timberwork

While the standard rectangular black timbers, infilled with white painted wattle and daub, were a common characteristic of Tudor houses, some skilled craftspeople went that extra mile with the wooden structure, introducing various repeating decorative elements. The result is often a striking house design that stands out from the norm.

TUDOR Interior Design

Showcase houses

If most houses were of simple design with little decoration, those of the wealthy showcased the work of the finest craftspeople – timber panelling in particular. Local timbers, mostly oak, were used with relatively small panels owing to the need to fashion them from planks, long before plywood was invented.

'Interior design' in the 21st century sense was in its infancy in Tudor times. The vast majority of houses were places of simple shelter and beautification of the interior was not a particularly high priority. However, the homes of the really wealthy were a different matter and houses such as Little Moreton Hall, in Cheshire, England, illustrate that fine craftsmanship was of interest to those who could afford it. The materials are spare – wood, wattle and daub infill, and rudimentary glazing (note the tiny pieces used as large panes could not be made at that time). However, the detail with which they were worked is exquisite, resulting in a house of real grandeur.

Fireplace focal point

The fireplace was the centre of every household, both as a source of heat and a place to cook and congregate around. If efforts were made to beautify a home, this is often where they were lavished. The surround most often featured a flat Tudor arch and simple, refined detailing, suited to the austere grandeur of this relatively recent innovation within the home.

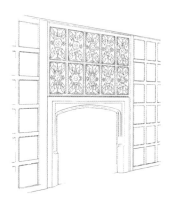

Not so much décor

Plain white internal walls, offset by rich, dark wooden beams – the style is unmistakable and has been copied throughout more recent architectural history. However, this simplicity of interior design was a necessity in Tudor times: the white panelling brightened up houses illuminated only by candlelight and a few small, often unglazed windows.

A simple aesthetic

Pendean Farmhouse in Sussex, England, is typical of rustic Tudor architecture of the 17th century. Its interior is dimly lit because there are only a few small windows. Walls on the first floor are clad in stone, while on the upper floor they are whitened wattle and daub, which contrasts with the heavy structural wooden beams.

Introduction

The Renaissance period is a very important one for house design. However, the style is pivotal not for the proliferation of houses built in this manner but for the influences taken from it. Renaissance architecture is, by virtue of its borrowing from ancient Greek and Roman style, a rather grand affair. In vogue between the 15th and 17th centuries throughout Europe, it originated in Italy and quickly spread to France, Germany and Russia.

Proponents of the style concentrated on symmetry, geometry and uniformity. They studied the ancient Greek temples, with their rows of identical columns and repetitive façades. As a result, houses that were built in the Renaissance style tend to be easy to spot, initially due to their attention to proportion and symmetry about a central line.

A classic example of this is Palazzo Farnese in Rome, Italy. The building, which today is the French Embassy, features row upon row of windows all of the same size, arranged about a central entrance arch. The design is symmetrical and beautifully proportioned, making for a grand building that is easy on the eye while still being awe-inspiring.

High design
One of the most important palaces in Rome, Palazzo Farnese was designed in 1517 and remodelled at a later date. Note the use of Classical elements, such as the different types of pediments capping the many windows and the central triumphal arch entrance.

Medici Villa di Poggio, otherwise known as Medicean Villa Ambra, is an important building within the history of Renaissance style. Designed by Giuliano da Sangallo and built between 1484 and 1520, the house was the summer residence of Lorenzo di Medici, a diplomat and politician, and one of a series of residences around Florence, Italy, owned by the family.

The villa is a prime example of the progression of the Renaissance style. References to ancient Greek and Roman architecture are made in the form of the series of semi-circular Romanesque arches at ground level and the large pediment, which sits above the glazed entrance at the top of the curving double staircase. The grandeur instilled by the two staircases matches that of the pediment, an element found on ancient Greek temples.

However, the sweeping style of the staircases, plus the giant, sculpted stone clock on the building's roof, champion the skills of an emerging breed of master builders, who would go on to influence architects over the next 300 years as much as those who built the Acropolis and Colosseum had done before them.

A grand entrance
The sweeping twin staircases of the Villa di Poggio reveal how the Renaissance style not only borrowed from the ancient but added its own twist to architecture's grand palette.

Archetypes

Italian origins

Set on a sloping hillside, Villa Medici di Fiesole in Tuscany is one of the oldest Renaissance houses in Italy. Both the house and the garden surrounding it are classic Renaissance in design, distinctive even after numerous renovations and additions throughout the property's five and a half centuries in existence.

The Renaissance style originated in Italy and the oldest and often finest examples of the genre can still be found there. One such house is the Villa Medici di Fiesole near Florence, which was designed by Michelozzo di Bartolomeo. Built in the 1450s, the house is square in plan and far less grandly adorned than villas of the same style. Its design illustrates the beginnings of the Renaissance, when designers such as di Bartolomeo, who were often sculptors and painters rather than purely architects, stuck rigidly to the tenets laid out by the ancient Greek and Roman builders. As time went by, designers began to impose their own flourishes on Renaissance period houses.

Typical design

Renaissance design has two very evident underlying traits. The first is symmetry. The second is a penchant for extravagant, Classically inspired decoration. Here, the archways, pediments, urn-shaped sculptures, and even a cupola on the roof all scream Renaissance design.

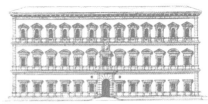

Repetition rules

The 16th-century Palazzo Farnese in Rome is a fine example of urban Renaissance design. While country villas tended towards flamboyance, those built within cities were often more staid. However, they were no less strict when it came the rule of symmetry.

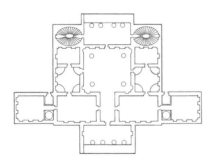

Planning symmetrically

Take a pencil and draw a line vertically down from the centre of the top of this plan view of one of Palladio's Italian villas and you'll see that the design of the villa is perfectly symmetrical. This trait was used not only in planning the layout of Renaissance houses but also on the façades, giving the houses a rigorous sense of order, underlying their often plentiful decoration.

Inside the Renaissance

This 15th-century sketch of the internal layout of the Gaddi family residence in Florence is interesting because it illustrates the intricacies of Renaissance design. Whereas Tudor houses had been simple structures, this 'new' style really began to test the builder's skill with many levels and complicated arrangements of rooms and circulation.

Archetypes

English style

The flat roof of The Queen's House in Greenwich, London, is unusual for a Renaissance building in continental Europe, but it was often used in Britain. Inigo Jones' design is indicative of the work of Palladio, one of the forefathers of Renaissance design, and typically it forgoes elaborate decoration in favour of a strict adherence to symmetry and proportion.

As the Renaissance flourished in Italy, artists and architects from different countries travelled there to study and learn the ways in which ancient Greek and Roman construction ideals were being revived and reinterpreted. One such traveller was Inigo Jones, who visited Italy late in the 1500s and brought back with him the knowledge to design some of England's first and ultimately finest Italian Renaissance-inspired buildings. A key example is The Queen's House in Greenwich. Now part of the National Maritime Museum, it was commissioned by King James I for Queen Anne of Denmark. The main house is flanked by long colonnades on both sides and is a wonderful example of Palladian architecture.

French twist

No nationality knows how to buck a trend beautifully more than the French. Here, a less than symmetrical example of French Renaissance style is indicated by traits including the Ionic capitals that top the pilasters on the façade, the Romanesque arch and the carved garlands.

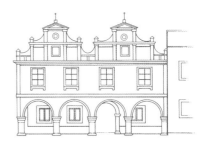

Czech style

A Renaissance house in Netolice, Czech Republic, has been turned into a museum for the town. Beautifully styled with an arched base and elaborately shaped gables at its top, surmounted by two pediments, this is a prime example of 16th-century northern European Renaissance design.

Dutch swagger

Bartolotti House is a red brick Dutch Renaissance house in Amsterdam built in 1615 by Hendrick de Keyser. It takes the style and goes completely over the top, with Roman urns, columns and other period decoration abounding. However, notice that everything is still symmetrical, providing order under this maelstrom of decoration.

Ornate German

Constructed during the latter years of the Renaissance, this house is reputed to be the oldest in Heidelberg, Germany. Its design is awash with sculptural flourishes but as with the similar Dutch Bartolotti House (left), the form and decoration is dictated by the symmetry so cherished by Renaissance designers.

Capra La Rotonda (1591)

Italian origins

Renaissance architecture has its roots in Italy and houses such as Villa Capra La Rotonda are the finest examples of High Renaissance architecture before it was adapted and watered down by architects intent on using elements of the style without sticking to its rigorous rules.

Capra La Rotonda is a Renaissance villa in Vicenza, northern Italy, designed by Andrea Palladio. Properly entitled 'Villa Almerico-Capra', the house is a UNESCO World Heritage Site and a beautiful example of the architect's work. Entirely symmetrical on all sides, the design revolves around a central circular hall, an indication of which can be seen in the central pitched roof. The villa is also positioned so that all its rooms will benefit from the sun at some point of the day. Palladio achieved this by rotating the building 45 degrees from a north–south axis. Both Palladio and the owner, Paolo Almerico, died before its completion, which was undertaken by Vincenzo Scamozzi.

Portico

The porticos of Capra La Rotonda, one on each of the four elevations of the villa, are an important stylistic element of the villa. Their design draws on the ancient Greek temple pediment and their scale gives this relatively modest Renaissance building a gravitas beyond its size or official importance.

Classical deities

The statues that stand proudly on top of the pediments on each of the four porticos all depict Classical deities. This trait is another indication of the ancient leanings of the Renaissance period, taking reference from both Greek and Roman sculptural tradition.

Plan view

No image illustrates the importance that Palladio and many other Renaissance architects placed upon symmetry better than this plan of Capra La Rotonda. The four entrances to the building lead through four corridors with identically proportioned rooms on each side, to a central circular hall.

Materials & Construction

Urban Renaissance

Designed by Baptiste du Cerceau for King Henry IV, there are 35 buildings that border the Place des Vosges in Paris, France. They were commissioned in 1604 and are indicative of the style of the time in France – tall and elegant with thin windows and restrained decoration.

Materials were important to the Renaissance architect but there was no defining type or immediately recognisable technique associated with the period. The reason is that design and construction techniques were becoming increasingly sophisticated and so architects and clients had a wider choice of materials to work with. At the Place des Vosges, a square in central Paris commissioned by Henri IV, the buildings that border it use a combination of red brick and white stone for their façades. The contrasting colours accentuate the Renaissance design and make for a most royal of spectacles.

Precise stonework

The Breakers, an 1895 mansion in Rhode Island, USA, was designed by Richard Morris Hunt. Its extravagant design, all in stone, is a prime example of wealthy Americans adopting the style of the European upper classes. The building is a testament to the stonemasons of the time and the amazing skill involved in creating heavily stylised stone masonry.

Tiled roofs

Renaissance-period houses almost invariably have tiled roofs. However, depending upon their location, these can be flat slates or curve- profile clay/ceramic tiles. For instance, in France – and Paris in particular – the trend was for grey slate on a steeply pitched roof, while in Italy a rural Renaissance villa would almost always be crowned with a low-pitched roof covered in red ceramic tiles.

Brickwork

Bricks were a material used predominantly in areas with little or no good stone to build with. Therefore, while southern Europe, including Italy, the home of Renaissance, designed and built in stone, houses in northern Europe were often constructed of brick, with stone used only as a decoration or accent in the design.

Cupolas

Domes abound on Renaissance cathedrals and can often be seen on houses too, especially those with a symmetrical plan. In addition, Renaissance designers also liked to top domes and towers with cupolas – a small windowed structure crowned with its own dome – that were designed to bring light into the top of the main dome.

Doors & Windows

As symmetry and proportion are such defining factors within Renaissance architecture, the positioning of windows and doors is of great importance to any Renaissance design, whether the building is a strict successor of ancient Greek models or a manipulated interpretation of Renaissance tenets. At Maison de La Boétie, a 16th-century house in Dordogne, France, the Italian Renaissance style is evident – note the heavily ornamented pilasters on the windows and gable decoration. Needless to say, the windows are aligned and their positioning is predictably 'correct' and in tune with the Renaissance ideals of the period.

Positioning

Even though this house is French, it is built in the Italian Renaissance style, and the location of openings in the façade is balanced aesthetically. The architect has considered the building's form and then placed the windows about a series of subtle centre lines. The complicated design makes the Renaissance ideals less obvious to all but the trained eye.

Variations in shape
The Rutzler, a house built in 1928 by
F. L. Bonfoey, in Charlotte, North Carolina,
features a variety of differently shaped
windows and frames. The rectangular
design is predominant but Roman arched
and pedimented windows are also included
in a design rich in Renaissance reference.

Romanesque arched doorways
Arches are often a good way of identifying
the influences of a building's design. In
Renaissance times the favoured arch was a
simple semicircular style, inspired by those
used in ancient Rome. If the top of the arch
is pointed, it is not Roman in descent but
Gothic. The variations are numerous.

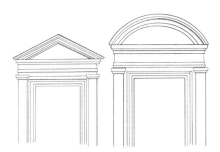

Angular and curved window pediments
Traditionally, pediments were the triangular
element above a row of columns at the
entrance to a temple, or similar. However,
Renaissance architects adapted them for
use above windows and they can be
triangular, curved and broken (when the
sculptural form is interrupted by a gap,
or often a statue).

Sculpted surrounds
Decoration was a major preoccupation
of Renaissance architects and sculpted
elements around windows and doors were
common. Often, the decoration included
pilasters (half columns) set in relief at
either side of the opening and travelling
upwards to give the impression of
supporting the cornice.

RENAISSANCE

Ornamentation

Rough Renaissance
Eildon Mansion was
originally known as
Barham House and since
its completion in 1850
it has housed rich
families, economy
backpackers and now a
French language school.
The building's richly
decorated façade is a
mix of rough rusticated
stones and smooth
stucco finish, making
a powerful architectural
statement.

Ornamentation and decoration come in many forms,
including decorative reliefs and ornamental pediments
discussed on pages 98–9). Other Renaissance traits
include the use of statues and other sculpted motifs,
especially urns, and decorative detailing at cornice
level and on pediments. However, rustication, the
practice of incorporating rough hewn stone into all or
a part of the building, is somewhat unusual on
Renaissance houses. Here, though, at Eildon Mansion
in St Kilda, Australia, architect John Gill used it to
great effect, the rusticated corner stones, or quoins,
accentuating the building's form and adding drama to
the front façade.

Contemporary take

New Islington is a housing scheme designed by British architectural practice FAT. It is unmistakably modern and yet the architect has opted to adorn the building façades with fancy shaped gables and to pick out the window surrounds in decorative white forms. This is a very contemporary take on Renaissance design.

Sgrafito decoration

Sgrafito, a technique of applying layers of coloured plaster to a wall to create a painted effect, was popular with Renaissance artists such as Polidoro da Caravaggio. German architects took the technique to northern Europe in the 16th century. Most original examples have now faded but newer works can be seen in Germany and Austria.

Unusual gable form

Drama and artistry, along with symmetry and proportion, were important in Renaissance design. Here, the wonderfully unique gable of this modest Dutch house exemplifies the sculptural excitement that some architects brought to the genre.

Use of sculpture

Its roots firmly ensconced in ancient Greek and Roman design, Renaissance architecture is awash with sculpture. Often single figures or friezes are incorporated, as are urns, a symbol synonymous with Roman times.

Interior Design

RENAISSANCE

Renaissance grandeur
Hardwick Hall in Derbyshire was designed by Robert Smythson. Its external symmetrical rigour turns into an interior of long and tall rooms bedecked with giant fireplaces, frescoes and ceilings bearing strapwork patterning and borders that include bands of anthemion, a stylised flower that first appeared in ancient Greek design.

The interiors of the later grand Renaissance houses of Europe were no less elaborately decorated than their glorious external façades. And, in the USA, Renaissance-inspired architecture went even further in its extravagance. Favourite decorative elements were heavily sculpted cornice details at the border of wall and ceiling, patterned ceilings and large carved fireplaces or other such focal points within expansive rooms. Structural elements were also exaggerated for decorative effect. Large multiple arches and fluted or smooth columns, adorned with composite and scroll-like Ionic capitals, often made appearances in the largest Renaissance houses.

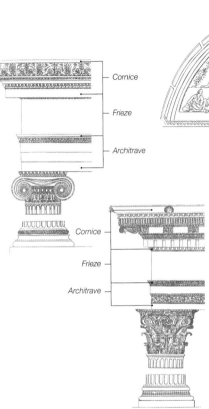

Frescoes

The practice of painting a series of related scenes to create a mural directly on the wall was one championed by Renaissance artists. At Medici Villa di Poggio, in Italy, frescoes by Allesandro Allori adorn many walls, often depicting historic or mythical figures and legends from Roman times.

Cornice

Frieze

Architrave

Cornice

Frieze

Architrave

Classical motifs (above)

The column, perhaps the most recognisable of historic construction elements, has been used throughout history, both as a structural device and decorative addition. Renaissance architects aped their ancient Roman counterparts and used columns and pilasters extensively within buildings to bring drama to room entrances.

Sculpted ornate balustrades

If the stairway is to be dramatic, then it must have a fancy balustrade. Made up of multiple curvaceously shaped balusters, the balustrades of Renaissance-era houses were perhaps the most elaborate of them all. Add to this a predilection for a sweeping curved staircase and the scene was set for Renaissance grandeur of the highest degree.

Introduction

Colonial architecture in the USA encompasses a variety of styles, each transported to the New World by settlers from Europe. The materials they used to build their homes on their arrival between the 16th and 19th centuries depended on what was available locally. However, whenever possible, the immigrants reverted to their known construction methods – the Dutch and English favouring stone or masonry over timber and the Spanish preferring to use adobe with a stucco finish.

These houses are especially interesting for their shape, a design quirk that settlers could maintain, even if they had to use a material type that was new to them. Here, the Spanish Customs House is a good example of French Colonial architecture blended with Caribbean influences. The veranda is often found on French Colonial houses, as are the small, yet tall, dormers in the roof. These features have been preserved by generations of architects and are still used today, mostly for sound architectural reasons – verandas allow outdoor living in warm, wet environments and small-windowed dormers prevent too much heat getting into the rooms of the upper floors.

French flair

The French built some of the most beautiful of colonial dwellings, many of which include large verandas and balconies, such as this one on the quirkily named Spanish Customs House at Lorriens Plantation, New Orleans. Settlers developed this style shortly after landing in the Mississippi Valley in the early 1700s.

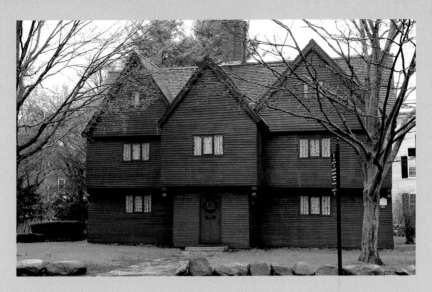

An Englishman's home
Corwin House is Colonial residential architecture at its best, showing how elements of the settlers' history were introduced into houses of the New World. It is perhaps rather bigger than most settlers could afford to build but the general principles of an English Colonial design were the same whether the house was for a wealthy man or a commoner looking to make a new life.

Corwin House (also called the Witch House, because of its owner's connection with the Salem Witch Trials of 1692) in Salem, Massachusetts, is a wonderfully preserved example of a First Period English house. Built for a wealthy judge, Jonathan Corwin, its design takes from the Tudor style in England, as can be seen by the steeply pitched roof line, triple casement windows and a large, centrally positioned chimney. Structurally, Corwin House is also reminiscent of its English counterparts, being built using post-and-beam construction, with a wood lath and plaster interior that gives it a remarkable Tudor feel. Contrasting these Tudoresque design elements is the outer façade of clapboard, which is undoubtedly not original and is very American in style.

Archetypes

German roots

Schifferstadt is a prime example of the home of a successful German immigrant farmer. Its size and number of rooms mark it out as far more than a first shelter built by newcomers. Usually, simple log cabins, *holzbau*, came first, followed by larger half-timbered dwellings named *fachwerkbau*. Finally, perhaps one or two generations later, came homes such as Schifferstadt.

The immigrant settlers in America came to make a better life for themselves and as they prospered they built bigger and more permanent homes. The building that is now the Schifferstadt Architectural Museum was once the home of Elias Bruner, the son of German settler Joseph Bruner. Elias built the house in 1758 using local sandstone from Walkersville, Maryland. However, the style of the house – solid stone walls, small windows, a steeply pitched roof – all date back to the houses of Joseph and Elias' German homeland. Another hint as to the provenance of this house and many others is its name. Joseph named his farm Schifferstadt after his hometown in the Palatinate region of southwest Germany.

Anglo-Dutch

John Bowne House, an Anglo-Dutch colonial dwelling built in Flushing, New York, in 1661, was designed to a Dutch plan, meaning that the house had gable ends to its roof, which sloped to a single storey at the rear, while being two storeys high at the front: a 'saltbox' design. Sloping dormers on the rear elevation enable the entire second storey to be used. Originally a simple rectangular plan, the house has been added to many times and now features extra wings to the west elevation.

English history

The Staten Island Peace Conference was held at this house on 11 September 1776. However, the modest front door marks out Conference House as a family home. While timber-framed houses were common in the 17th century, stone houses were built by the wealthy; this one is in an English Colonial style.

Double Dutch

The double-pitched, or gambrel, roof is a clear indication that John Teller House is a Dutch Colonial home. Built in the Stockade neighbourhood of Schenectady, New York State, in the 1740s, its brick construction and the two matching chimneys are also clues as to the origin of its builder.

Simple Spanish

The Avila Adobe in Los Angeles was built in 1818 by Francisco Jose Avila, a former mayor of the city. The use of adobe was indicative of Mediterranean-style houses being built by settlers. In its time it has been a restaurant, boarding house and a house, and is now a museum, displaying artefacts from the 1800s.

Archetypes

Dutch Revival

The gambrel roof and stone-clad lower storey of this house inspired by Dutch colonial dwellings have been combined with a somewhat extravagant columned portico, which would be more at home on a Neoclassical house. Still, the history behind this revival house shows through in the design.

In the USA some of the most popular revivalist architectures for houses of a modest nature are not Renaissance or Neoclassical but Colonial. Here, a relatively new house still clearly references Dutch architectural features brought to America in the 1600s–1700s, in its roof shape, materials and even window positioning. The reason for this harking back to history is unclear with many newer houses but an educated guess is that people tend to like what they know and so an architect is likely to be more successful in presenting a design such as this, as opposed to one so new and radical that it sets a new precedent.

Spanish Revival

The East Alvarado Historic District in Phoenix, Arizona, has a small set of houses now protected due to their architectural significance. This Spanish Revival Colonial house was the first to be built in a new trend that swept the region in the 1920s. Its arches, stucco façade and red tile roof give it a look typical of colonial houses built hundreds of years before.

French Revival

This new house in Pensacola, Florida, designed by architect Cooper Johnson Smith, is almost a carbon copy of many French colonial houses of the late 1700s and early 1800s. Its architecture is inspired as much by historic traits designed to make for comfortable living in the southern states as by any Euro-French aspirations. Houses from the period, looking remarkably like this new one, can still found today.

German Colonial Revival

This simple little dwelling could be the generic child's drawing of a house but its roots can be traced back to German Colonial architecture. The symmetry of the façade, steeply sloping gabled roof and pediment above the centre window are indications of the style that influenced this contemporary house.

English Colonial Revival

Black and white, with strict rectangular windows and a central front door, this house has many attributes of an English, or First Period, Colonial house. The shutters on the windows and rather grand porch allude to other styles favoured by Americans looking to capture the essence of historic residential architecture.

The Old Stone House (1740)

The Old Stone House, built in around 1740 in Richmond, Virginia, is home to the Edgar Allan Poe Museum. The house was in fact never home to Poe but it holds a large collection of his manuscripts. Built by Jacob Ege, a German immigrant, the house's design illustrates the German penchant for thick stone walls and small windows. After Ege's death it was owned by his son and it remained in the family until 1911. Preservation Virginia saved the house from demolition soon after, and in 1921 it was announced that it would be the home of the shrine to Edgar Allan Poe.

An old stone house
Diminutive from the street, the Old Stone House is deep in plan and includes a walled garden to the rear. Its second storey, within the gabled roof, provides a surprising amount of space for the museum exhibits and the house draws thousands of visitors each year.

Garden cloister

Unusually for any house, let alone a colonial home of the 18th century, the Old Stone House has a cloister in its back garden. The small covered walkway with semicircular brickwork arches houses a shrine (a bust of Poe).

Dormer windows

Typical of historic German residential architecture, the dormer windows in the gabled roof of the Old Stone House are utilitarian in nature. They do not include the sloping accents of Dutch styling or the eyebrow lintels so often found on English houses of the period.

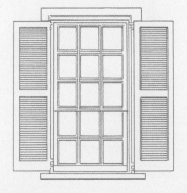

Shuttered window

Shutters were common on colonial houses of all types in the 17th and 18th centuries, purely because they gave protection against the weather for often unglazed window openings. These simple battened shutters add little decoration but they are true to the house's colonial roots.

Materials & Construction

Stucco façade

Stucco is a wet wall covering, made of lime, sand, animal or plant fibres (for strength) and water. The ingredients are mixed together into a sticky consistency that allows the builder to apply it to the wall with a trowel. The covering is trowelled reasonably flat and left to dry and harden into a durable external covering.

Adobe block walls and a stucco-rendered façade covering are a common sight in many African, Mediterranean and South American regions. The simple construction techniques work well in hot countries because the clay bricks and wet applied render both use the sun to bake them hard and make them durable. Here, the Gonzalez Alvarez House is an example of part-adobe and part-timber frame design, built in St Augustine, Florida, in the 16th century. The erstwhile home is now owned by the St Augustine Historical Society and is open for public tours.

Wrap-around veranda

The wrap-around veranda on this French colonial house in Missouri shaded the walls and interior from the heat of the day and made for a great place to sit and enjoy the evening under cover. The construction type is called *poteaux en terre* (posts in ground), referring to the wooden columns that support the house.

Tiled roofs

Tiles come in many forms but those used predominantly by Spanish and some French settlers tended to be the shaped clay tiles that were employed back in their homelands. These tiles were relatively easy to make with a little experience and they could be baked from local materials such as clay.

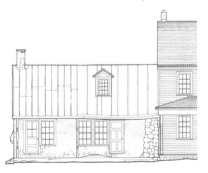

Timber construction

Lighter to build and using a material that was to be found growing almost everywhere in the first settlements, timber-framed and clad houses were often the first option for new settlers. From log cabin to clapboard house, the timber-framed house has always been, and still remains, an indelible part of American residential architectural history.

Solid stone walls

While certain immigrants favoured timber construction techniques, the Germans and British tended towards heavier building methods, and none is more robust than the solid stone wall. Often several feet thick, these walls kept the interior cool, even during summer, and required almost no maintenance.

Doors & Windows

English oddity

Wells-Thorn House in Franklin County, Massachusetts, is odd insofar as its design is very much First Period Colonial, with Georgian-style windows and door positioning and little adornment of the frames. However, the timber construction is atypical, probably because no stone or brick was available locally.

Doors and windows can provide many clues to a house's architectural roots – from the shape of the arch to the positioning of the openings in the house's façade – one simply has to know how to read them. While structures such as log cabins were purely utilitarian, settlers often went on to design and build houses in the style they were used to. English immigrants in the 17th and 18th centuries tended towards symmetrical designs with lots of windows, following the Georgian style. The Spanish, on the other hand, preferred fewer windows and asymmetrical positioning.

Louvred

Solid board and batten

Flat or raised panel

Shuttered windows

Shutters were an often-used item on colonial houses, enabling occupants to keep out the weather, be it hot or cold and wet. Different shutter designs were favoured by different settlers: the Spanish tended to use solid board and batten shutters, the Dutch and English flat or raised panel designs, while the French opted for louvred shutters to allow a breeze through.

Making a point

If ever there were a statement-making decorative architectural addition, it has to be the porch, portico or pediment. This triangular pediment is sourced straight from ancient Greek architecture. The message is: 'Take this house seriously because it has historic references.' Hopefully, the pediment and portico are tastefully presented and not oversized as on some Neoclassical houses.

Door surrounds

The surround to the front door is not an important element within a house's construction. However, features such as narrow windows on either side of the door point to a Georgian design and provide a possible hint about the ancestry of the house's original occupants.

A hole in the wall

Windows (their number, position and shape) tell us a good deal about a house's design. However, first and foremost they are about allowing light into the house. Here, however, there comes a dilemma – more light means bigger holes in the façade, which means more exposure to weather. Northern European settlers tended to favour small windows to keep out the cold, while Spanish and other Mediterranean immigrants preferred bigger windows.

Ornamentation

English/American mix
The porch on Valentine
Varian House is of
Georgian styling – the
simple smooth-faced
columns supporting a
Classical triangular
pediment. However, the
fact that it is made from
wood rather than stone
makes it very American
in construction and so
a combination of two
architectural cultures.

Once the necessary structural and spatial elements of
a house's design have been attended to, it is time to
add a little character in the form of ornamentation.
Renaissance and Neoclassical houses are renowned for
ornamentation, but Colonial houses often kept this
kind of extravagance to a minimum, probably because
of the limited funds of many settlers in the New World.
However, each group of immigrants brought with them
certain quirks that can be readily identified. Valentine
Varian House in New York city is strongly representative
of the Georgian Colonial house, the raised-panel
shutters and gabled porch being the only real added
extras on the house's façade.

Spanish arches

Arches, in windows, doorways or as a support for covered verandas and porches, were highly favoured by Spanish immigrants. In form, these arches are predominantly semicircular, descendants of the Romanesque round arch, which was used as much for its structural qualities as its good looks.

Dutch porch

Many Dutch Colonial dwellings feature a prominent porch or portico over the front door, in contrast to the majority of English and German houses of the period. While some porches were minimal affairs, many were an excuse to make a statement and often incorporated Classical features such as broken pediments and scrolled columns.

French dormer

French colonial houses often had very shallow hipped roofs, as opposed to the steeply pitched gabled type of German houses. In order to make use of the roof space, dormer windows were added to allow in light. These dormers also added character and some were even scaled up to create extra architectural drama.

German stoicism

Stereotypes tend to arise because there is always some truth hidden somewhere within them. And so it is with German colonial architecture: immigrants eschewed ornamentation in favour of regimented style, such as symmetry of windows on a façade and rectangular house plans rather than the rambling Spanish style of house.

Interior Design

Interior design was, like external decoration, an afterthought for most new settlers. However, each style of house has its own defining internal characteristics and it is these that help to place colonial houses within their specific genre. Over time, houses began to become more grand, exhibiting increasingly lavish interior design. However, in the 17th and 18th centuries, houses were first and foremost functional, with form being a secondary consideration. The fireplace was the centre of the home, the walls and ceilings bore testament to the construction techniques used to build the house, and furniture was sparse due to limited space or money.

Timber-framed décor
The Stanley-Whitman House in Farmington, Connecticut, built *c.* 1720, is now a museum of the colonial era and a wonderfully preserved period house. The timber construction can be seen plainly in the walls and the ceilings, where posts, beams and boards are exposed to the interior. Notice the width of the floorboards, cut from old growth trees, the size of which is hardly ever seen today.

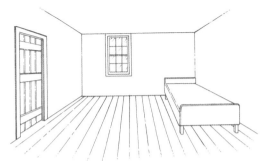

Bare necessities

Colonial houses often had little more furniture in them than was absolutely necessary. That meant a table and chairs, plus shelves for cooking utensils in the kitchen-cum-living area; and, upstairs, beds, a place to sit and somewhere to put the wash basin.

Fireplace focal point

The fireplace was the focal point of the home, both because it kept people warm and because it was used for cooking. Within the fireplace of many houses was an oven, which consisted of a small alcove, often with an arched roof. Items such as bread could be put into this and baked using the direct heat of the fire.

A school room

Within the confined space of this late 17th-century Dutch dwelling, called Voorlezer's House, was a schoolroom. This is unusual but not unknown elsewhere because the *voorlezer* is the lay minister and teacher for the community and his home also served as a church until another building could be constructed.

Introduction

A simple symmetrical style

With the Georgian era came a restraint not seen in architecture since the beginnings of the Renaissance. Decoration was stripped away and formality returned to designs. Windows were set in rows, doors positioned centrally in façades and roofs with paired chimneys crowned symmetrical-styled houses.

Georgian architecture covers the period between 1720 and around 1840, during which England had four kings named George. The style is derivative of Palladian architecture, meaning that Georgian architects were very interested in symmetry and proportion. Houses of the period would usually feature a central front door bordered on either side by matching numbers of windows. Chimneys, instead of rising from a central position in the roofline as in Tudor times, would be paired, rising from either end of the roof.

A fine example of this is Stockerston Hall in Leicestershire, England, shown here. Built in 1800, the house's low-pitched, hipped roof is typical of the Georgian style, as are the 12-pane sash windows.

These windows were never paired, as can be seen in other genres such as Victorian architecture, and often got smaller in the upper storeys of the house, where the servants lived. Notice also the stone lintels above the windows and the matching stone quoins at the corner of the house. These adornments are restrained and nicely proportioned, as all good Georgian architectural elements should be.

Georgian architecture extended beyond large farm houses and stately homes and entered into the urban environment. Often large terraces of Georgian houses can be seen in big cities in the UK and, in countries with English influence, the genre has also pervaded everyday life.

Take, for example, Elfreth's Alley in Philadelphia, Pennsylvania. Reputed to be one of America's oldest continuously inhabited residential streets, the rows of small houses, built between 1728 and 1836 along either side of it, are wonderful examples of down-to-earth Georgian architecture.

With two-storey houses on one side and three-storey on the other, Elfreth's Alley has been occupied by immigrants of many different nationalities during its existence. However, what has remained unchanged is the style of house. Neat six-panel doors and 12- or 15-pane windows line the street. The shutters, typically brightly painted, are raised panel – an English favourite – which matches the doors. The brickwork is English bond and the cornices adorning the roof lines and some of the lower storeys are suitably refined in their moulding – not overly worked, as was the penchant in Renaissance times.

Alley-style architecture
Elfreth's Alley is a great snapshot of English period architecture transposed to the USA. The street would slot into any British city almost unnoticed.

Archetypes

Old English

The design of Saltram House in Devon, now owned by the National Trust, exemplifies the Georgian aesthetic. Two storeys of large windows line the façade, with a smaller band above for the servants' quarters. The large pediment at roof level references ancient Greek designs, a nod to the influence of the forefathers of architecture.

Even the most archetypal of archetypes can hide a secret and there are plenty buried in the walls and interiors of Saltram House, near Plymouth, England. While the house looks very Georgian today, it began life as a Tudor building, but was subsequently altered and added to by a succession of owners over a period of almost a century between the mid-1700s and 1800s. Today, Saltram is considered a fine example of an early Georgian house. The various architects who worked upon it, including Robert Adam, have instilled a symmetry to the façade and restrained from overly adorning the exterior with too many Renaissance-like tweaks and twirls.

Canadian similarities

The Grange, a Georgian manor house in downtown Toronto, Canada, could be a carbon copy of the house of an affluent English farmer. Built in 1817 for D'Arcy Boulton, the house was the first home of the Art Museum of Toronto. It is now part of the Art Gallery of Ontario.

Australian influence

Juniper Hall, in Sydney, Australia, shows English architecture gone native. The combination of period architecture and necessity – the shady balconies on the main façade – elevates the house from an English transplant to the colonies into an important progression of architectural style to suit the very different climate of southern Australia.

Irish grandeur (left)

Ireland has its fair share of stately homes and Kilcolman Rectory in County Cork is one of them. Beautifully proportioned, from the arch of the front door to the brooding masses of the chimneys, the house is a masterclass in the quiet splendour that the best Georgian houses possess.

American style

Westover, a plantation house in the James River valley, Virginia, is a colonial house and an American twist on Georgian design. The chimneys are paired at each end of the house but rise to a height much greater than would be considered appropriate on an English house of the period. The roof, bedecked with dormers, is grandiose but another indication of Georgian architecture.

Archetypes

High society

Georgian rigour meets Renaissance flair in London's Belgrave Square. The rectangular shape and reduction in size of the windows in the higher storey point to Georgian designs, but the composite capitals on the columns and Roman urns on the roof indicate earlier influences often referenced by Georgian architects too.

Georgian architecture had a regimented rigour about it that no previous style possessed. As such, it made for a wonderful medium in which to design and build terraced houses. This type of house was taken to its grandest in London, in the early 1800s, when Belgrave Square was built. Three terraces of 11 and one of 12 houses lined the square, all designed by architect George Basevi. The four-storey terraces included all of the usual Georgian traits plus ancient flourishes, such as the Roman urns that line their parapets. The resulting homes now house international embassies and esteemed colleges.

Middle-class homes (left)
This row of middle-class houses is typical of almost any urban centre in the UK. Georgian to a fault, it is devoid of unnecessary decoration and laid out with a particular emphasis on repetition and uniformity. This is what Georgian architecture was all about and one of the reasons it has endured.

Working-class homes
The working classes were also treated to Georgian design, albeit on a much reduced scale than that of the London terraced mansions. Here, the house on the left still has its multiple-paned windows, while they have been replaced by a more Victorian style on the house to the right. Both feature a Roman arch over the doorway.

Australian uniformity (left)
As if plucked from a city backstreet in England, this terrace in New South Wales, Australia, illustrates the colonial influence that architectural styles display. The only relief that these small houses have is the cornice at roof level – an indication of architectural thought where all else is utilitarian normality.

Keats House (1815)

The house next door
John Keats' home was in the small attachment to the larger Regency-style house. Its hidden roof line and prominent chimney detract from Georgian qualities such as the large 15-paned windows, which admitted plenty of light to Keats at his desk.

Keats House, or Wentworth Place as it was originally known, was the London house in which English poet John Keats resided during the latter part of his life. The house is of Regency style, a derivative of classical Georgian architecture, which developed in the latter years of George III's monarchy. The house was not built for Keats, he merely rented the smaller part for a little under two years. The Brawne family – Fanny Brawne was his fiancée at the time of his early death – lived in the larger, grander part of the house. The house, now a museum to Keats, is open to the public.

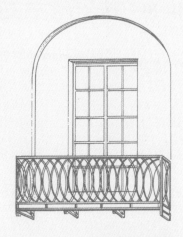

Window and wrought-iron balcony

The rectangular window within a recessed flattened arch is of tasteful Georgian design. The wrought-iron balcony in front of the window is an added touch that marks this house out as being of Regency style. Ironwork such as this is a classic trait of the latter Georgian years – 1815 onwards.

Fanlight and plaque

A minor detail or nicely executed Georgian trait? The semicircular fanlight over the main door to the house may not look much but it is another indication of Georgian restraint and style. Above it is a plaque installed by the Society of Arts to commemorate Keats' short but productive life.

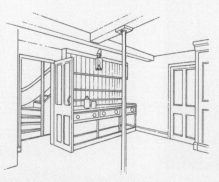

Basement life

While the rooms above were decorated to suit the pocket of a relatively well-off family in the early 19th century, the kitchen in the basement was, by contrast, a functional space with no frills. A large dresser serves to hold plates and pots and pans, while a fireplace and bread oven offer cooking facilities for the servants.

Materials & Construction

Georgian houses were constructed predominantly out of either stone or brick, depending upon their location and the wealth of the owner. Many larger houses were also finished in white stucco plaster. There is evidence of timber Georgian dwellings in America but even here the timber cladding was often designed to look like stone. If a house combined brick and stone, it tended to use stone for the lower storey, or accentuated the house's lines with stone quoins on the corners of the building or stone cornices that split the brickwork storeys of the façade. Details at the roof cornice were often of carved stone, and were duplicated on lower cornice bands. The roof of a Georgian house was almost always relatively low pitched and covered in flat tiles or slates.

A brick palace
The Derby House in Salem, Massachusetts, is a prime example of Georgian architecture in America. Clad in brick, it features windows with no fewer than 24 panes in them. The pediment above the front door matches the outer two dormers, while the centre one is curved – an architect's characterful twist.

Stone favourite

Stone was a favourite material of Georgian architects in England and houses were designed either with exposed stone façades or stucco-covered stone. In America stone was also used but more often brick was the material of choice. Alternatively, wood was used, as it was far less expensive and more readily available.

Tasteful rustication

The Georgian House Museum, in Bristol, is a nice example of how English architects used rustication to accentuate one storey while those above are left clean and so feel lighter aesthetically. The heavy lines of the rustication give the sense of large stone blocks: a trait seen on many Georgian houses and those of other styles, too.

Three storeys tall

The archetypal size for a Georgian house is not fixed but many were built to be three storeys high, with an additional basement level. The first two storeys above ground were for the main occupants while the upper floor, often in the roof, was for servants. The basement often had a kitchen, scullery and other work-related spaces.

Low-pitched roof

Georgian houses very seldom had steeply pitched roofs. Architects, taking from the Palladian ideals that stressed proportion above all other, kept roofs of low pitch so as not to detract from the beautiful symmetry of the main façade.

Doors & Windows

Built in the Federal style, an American incarnation of Georgian architecture, the Merchant's House is an early 19th-century family home in New York that has been preserved intact. The front façade is not quite symmetrical – the door being on the right – but the alignment of windows and the framing of the doorway in a Roman arch both allude to the period. The façade has three storeys of 12-paned windows plus roof dormers where the servants would have lived. These dormers, along with the front door, display an extravagance not usually seen in Georgian architecture in Europe.

Regimented rigor

Menard Lafever designed the Merchant's House, which was built in 1832. While a Victorian dwelling would have numerous sizes and forms of window, this Federal-style building had three floors with windows of identical size and shape opening. Only the uppermost storey had smaller windows.

Small-paned windows

Georgian houses typically have windows with multiple small panes because the method of manufacturing glass at the time was to blow a globe and then spin it to make a flat circular pane. This was quite small and so windowmakers built frames with lots of little openings for glass cut from these pieces.

Dormer pediments

Inspired by Classical architecture, Georgian designers used elements such as pediments to adorn their buildings. A favoured trait was to top dormer windows on the same roof with differently shaped pediments, say two triangular ones on either side of a curved one, all the while ensuring that the design was symmetrical.

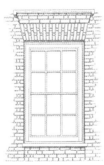

Brickwork detailing to openings

The Georgian period saw perhaps the height of the championing of brickwork and many houses featured clever, and often subtle, use of the material. Arches, curved or flat, provided strength to support the wall above and elongate the window, accentuating the verticality of the design.

Fanlight above entrance

Fanlights, the small windows above the entrance door, allow light into the hall of a house. In Georgian times they were often arched in design – a semicircular arch, taken from Roman tradition. Fanlights were almost always split into sections and panes via decorative metal frames.

Ornamentation

Rusticated façade
The entire first-floor façade of the original main houses built on the north side of Grosvenor Square was clad in a rusticated finish. The over-emphasised stone blocks and joints served to link the houses visually and contrasted with the vertical accentuation of the pilasters running up the façade of the central property.

From the early Georgian period onwards uniform rows of houses – terraces – were designed and built in London. The style lent itself to repetition on a grand scale, and to creating processional architecture often with a central flourish in the form of Classically accented adornments. One of the most famous Georgian squares, some parts of which still stand today, is Grosvenor Square in Mayfair, where since 1785 the American Embassy, in one form or another, has been located. The original houses in Grosvenor Square were three storeys high, with a basement below and small servants' quarters above. Decoration was kept to a minimum apart from the central house, which has a row of pilasters rising through the second and third floors, with an arched façade below.

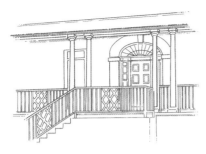

Australian additions

Cleveland House is a prime example of a Georgian design being adapted to suit the climate in which it is built. The 1824 house is located in Sydney, Australia, and while a veranda is not typical of Georgian architecture, it serves to shade the interior of the house and create a place for occupants to sit outside during the warm evenings.

Classically inspired pilasters

Pilasters are faux columns; adornments with capitals and bases similar to columns but with no structural significance. They were often used by Georgian architects to differentiate specific parts of a building, usually the central portion, and to add drama to the restrained, almost plain style.

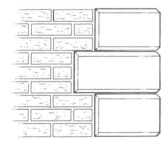

Stone quoins

Regularly shaped blocks of stone were used both decoratively and as reinforcement to the corners of brick and stone walls. These stone blocks or quoins are particularly noticeable where an architect twins white stone with red brickwork. The design accentuates the corner of the wall, be it on the main façade or at a window opening.

Oddities

For every rule there is an exception. This house, of Georgian origin (note the window details, main entrance with curved fanlight and shallow-pitched hipped roof) features a dramatic bow window that creates an alcove over the front door. The result is unique, if not to the taste of every aficionado of Georgian architecture.

Interior Design

Period splendour

The Georgian House Museum in Bristol, has rooms decorated in period style. The emphasis is still on symmetry around a central point, here the fireplace. Furniture is understated and refined, a foil to the decorative finish of the fireplace.

While Georgian design was not as flamboyant as some of its predecessors or successors, it was by no means their inferior. A middle- to upper-class Georgian house featured decorative fireplaces, arched entrances and well-executed cornice details that created an air of grandeur without going over the top, as could often be the problem with Renaissance interior design. Additionally, a dado rail – a wooden moulding running around the wall at a height corresponding to the height of a chair back – may have been installed, to protect the wall from being rubbed and damaged by chairs.

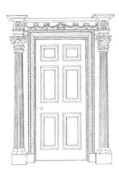

Internal columns

Borrowing from ancient Rome and Greece, Georgian architects and interior designers used columns as sentries, marking entrance ways between rooms. They were often coupled with an arch – flattened if in a modest house, Romanesque if a feature of a larger property.

Ornamented fire surrounds

The focal point of the room since our cave-dwelling ancestors, the fireplace still held the attention of people in Georgian times. The surround was often the most impressive furniture element within a room. Mini columns or pilasters were common, supporting a Classical entablature, as seen on ancient Greek temples.

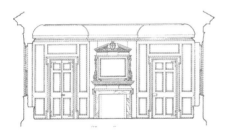

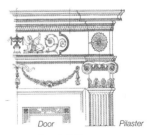

Door   Pilaster

Wood wall panelling

Wooden wall panelling was more commonly used in rural houses than their urban counterparts. It was sometimes extended to the full height of the wall but often restricted to the lower part, where it protected the wall against damage from chairs. Panels were generally square at the lowest level and rectangular above.

Heavy cornice details

Mouldings are a favourite of Georgian designers, especially the cornice moulding around the perimeter of the ceiling. As with other decorative elements, designers took their lead from Classical architecture and often used the acanthus leaf or egg and dart motifs.

Introduction

Marble masterpiece
The construction of Vanderbilt Marble House sparked a building boom in the sleepy neighbourhood of Newport, Rhode Island, which was transformed over the next half century from a colony of wooden cottages into a collection of grand mansions. In fact, the entire Bellevue Avenue Historic District is now designated a National Historic Landmark.

While Georgian architecture still reigned supreme in England, other European countries were reacting against the predominant Rococo and Baroque styles. The prevailing genre was that of Neoclassicism, or Federal architecture as the style was termed in the United States.

Neoclassical design shunned the naturalistic sculpture favoured by Baroque fans and the overemphasis on structural elements that Renaissance architecture tended towards. Instead, like Georgian design, it looked to the Classical model, that of ancient Roman and Greek architecture, for inspiration.

Vanderbilt Marble House, built on Rhode Island, USA in 1892, was designed by Richard Morris Hunt for railroad baron William K. Vanderbilt and it is considered one of the USA's finest examples of Neoclassical architecture. The stone façade of this landmark mansion is resplendent with fluted Greek pilasters, bedecked with Corinthian capitals. Similarly, the fluted columns and acanthus leaf-covered capitals that support the portico are of ancient Greek inspiration.

Neoclassicism came to the UK through a series of grand stately homes built by wealthy families. Kedleston Hall in Derbyshire is one such home. It was designed by James Paine and Matthew Brettingham. Both men were inspired by Palladian design but in the midst of their work the commission was stripped from them and given to a young Robert Adam – who would go on to become one of England's most celebrated Neoclassical architects.

House style

Kedleston Hall in Derbyshire, England, was designed initially in Palladian style but was completed to Neoclassical designs. The extravagant Corinthian portico that can be seen here was a stylistic gesture by Robert Adam, the architect who completed the house after others had started it. The addition does not detract from the grandeur of a home that was originally designed to be less visually ornate.

Adam took Brettingham and Paine's designs and completed them much as they were originally drawn. However, he took the liberty of making his personal statement in the form of a dramatic Corinthian-styled portico addition to the north elevation and by adding a blind triumphal arch, based on the Arch of Constantine in Rome, to the south façade.

The interior is no less impressive. Entry from the north takes visitors down a marble hall lined with columns, which leads to the south end of the house where the saloon, a room 19 m (62 ft high), is crowned with a dome and a glass oculus (skylight). The design of Kedleston Hall is completed by majestic gardens dotted with other Neoclassical buildings and bridges, also designed by Adam.

Archetypes

Euro chic

Neglecting the flamboyant design often seen in American Neoclassical houses, the Casita del Principe near Madrid is a study in proportion, its upper storey and associated wings deferring to the main volume of the building.

Neoclassicism took on different forms, or trends, depending upon where it was practised. The Casita del Principe, a summer house for the heir to the Spanish throne, Charles, Prince of Asturias, was designed by architect Juan de Villanueva in 1784. The house forgoes the grand double-height portico in favour of a single storey entrance with an ornate wrought-iron balcony above. Notice the difference in column design between first and second storey – on the first the columns are Tuscan (you can tell by the capitals and plain frieze above) while the scrolled capitals of the upper storey are of Ionic design.

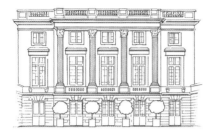

French restraint

Petit Trianon, by Neoclassical architect
Ange-Jaques Gabriel, is a small château
in the grounds of the Palace of Versailles,
southwest of Paris. It is square in plan and
each of the four façades is designed slightly
differently depending upon what their
outlook is. Gabriel used Corinthian order
columns and pilasters and adorned the roof
with a heavy stone balustrade.

All things Classical

The Charles O. Robinson House, in
Elizabeth City, North Carolina, is a great
example of Neoclassicism gone crazy. The
house's dramatic portico extends out over
a lower wrap-around veranda and both
are supported by multiple Classical columns.
Dormers with triangular pediments appear
at every space on the roof and the cornices
of both storeys are intricately detailed.

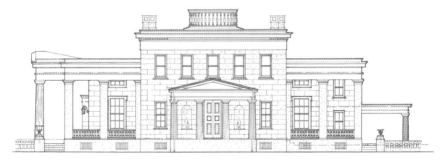

Greek Revival

With columns lining its main façade and
a giant, yet simply designed pediment
crowning the portico, this house is modelled
on ancient Greek temples. This aspect of
Neoclassical architecture is termed Greek
Revival, and was popular in the USA
during the mid-19th century.

Archetypes

Neoclassicism is an enduring style and one still practised by some architects. The firm Robert Adam Architects has designed Solar House, an environmentally friendly house in Sussex, that exemplifies the genre. Its columned portico sports a broken pediment that allows low sunlight into the main hall in the winter but shades it in the summer. Two pediment-topped wind towers, high on the roof, suck out warm stale air from the upper storey, thereby drawing in cool fresh air at a lower level. The windows on the southern façade admit plenty of natural light but are also proportioned as those in a Classical building would be, working perfectly with the proportions of the rest of the building.

Classical green

Although not often attempted, the combination of environmental design and Classical architecture can be achieved, as in this country house in Sussex. It should come as no surprise because the ancient Greeks and Romans did not have air conditioning or artificial lighting as we know it and so had to light and cool their buildings passively, just as architects are now attempting to do once again.

Small scale

Neoclassical architecture is often regarded as something for the stately home, mansion house or château, but even a small bungalow can incorporate some stately grandeur courtesy of Tuscan order columns and gables that allude to the pediments of ancient Greece.

A hint of...

Some would call this house a Georgian design and they may well be right, but every house is different and the unusual columned entrance, plus a broken pediment at the roof line point to Neoclassical pretensions.

Over the top

The phrase 'less is more', adopted by Modernist architect Mies van der Rohe, obviously didn't enter the head of the designer of this house. The circular portico, complete with Composite order columns and a heavily moulded cornice, completely overpowers the more restrained design of the house itself.

Monticello (1796)

Home for a president
Jefferson constructed a two-storey building initially, before tearing down the upper floor in 1796 and rebuilding what we see today, according to a new design. The former president died in debt and the house was sold to a local apothecary who unsuccessfully used the estate to farm silkworms.

Designing for himself, the third President of the United States, Thomas Jefferson, built and rebuilt his house, named Monticello, over a number of years between 1769 and 1808. Jefferson designed the house according to Neoclassical principles, drawing upon the works of Andrea Palladio. The porticoed elevations are immediately recognisable as Neoclassical – with the columns and pediment dominating. However, note the symmetry of the overall design, and the domed roof, a particular favourite of ancient Roman builders for public buildings. The arched windows in some areas and semicircular fanlights are also striking.

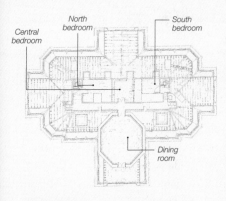

Central bedroom

North bedroom

South bedroom

Dining room

Plan of layout

Even though the building's plan isn't a mirror image if split in two, its form, as well as the layout of the load-bearing walls, adheres to Classical rules of symmetry. Jefferson was clever enough to design a functional house that remained true to his architectural beliefs.

The dome

The dome that crowns Monticello is a wonderful example of how Neoclassicism borrows from ancient Rome. The stepped external construction and the coffered ceiling are similar to the Pantheon, built in Rome in AD 126. Monticello's Dome Room is only a single storey high though, not the grand high-ceilinged central space as imagined from outside.

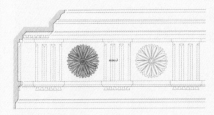

Internal cornices

The heavy cornices that adorn the ceiling edge in many of the rooms feature differing motifs. In the tea room the cornice decoration alternates between miniature triple pilasters and rosettes – stylised flowers – a common Classical design.

External cornice and balustrade

The external cornice is similar in style to that within the dining room and above it a relatively slender balustrade caps the brick walls and borders the pitched roof, which is set back from the walls and is today clad in a metal standing-seam finish.

Materials & Construction

Material contrast
The Woodlands, in
Philadelphia, uses the
contrast between the
rough hewn stone and
smooth white columns
of its two-storey portico
to accentuate elements
of the Neoclassical
design. The finishing
touches include windows
within Roman arches,
again emphasizing the
design flourishes of this
extravagant house.

Neoclassical houses tend to be built from stone or brick – the former directly correlating with the materials used in ancient Classical construction and the latter having some connection to the earth and Old World techniques. In addition, construction styles often aim to mimic the work of Greek and Roman craftsmen, even if the actual technique used is far more modern and energy-efficient. A case in point relates to the manufacture of external cornices. Originally these would have been carved from stone; today cornices are manufactured in concrete or other lighter materials, making them quicker and easier to create and install.

The portico

The portico is an important part of the Neoclassical house, especially in houses built in the USA. Elsewhere it is sometimes forgotten but in America the portico is seen as the pivotal element in a design of this genre. Some designs take it to the extreme and include giant, sometimes overstated, entrances in an attempt to proclaim their Neoclassical credentials.

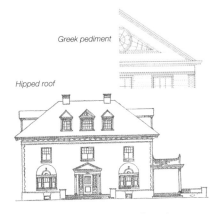

Greek pediment

Hipped roof

Hipped roofs and Greek pediments

The hipped roof and Greek pediment go hand in hand, as the pediment acts as a stone buffer to the gabled front façade of a Classical temple roof. Where this pediment is neglected, the hipped roof provides a well-proportioned crown to a house designed along Classical lines.

Rustication

Rustication is used to accentuate particular parts of a building. It is also a nod to ancient times when rough stone was used to build with. Today, rusticated blocks are often cast from concrete, rather than being sourced from quarries – both for their relative uniformity and lower cost.

Wooden twist

For every typical design within a style there is an unusual counterpoint. Here, a modern timber-clad house has been designed to include a full-length double-height canopy, supported by slender columns and sporting a type of triangular pediment. The result is ungainly but the aspirations are evident.

NEOCLASSICAL Doors & Windows

Unquestionably doors and windows are important parts of any building. However, few architectural styles celebrate the entrance to a house as extravagantly as Neoclassical design. The reason for this is the style's preoccupation with Classical motifs and grand structures such as the temples and political edifices of ancient Rome and Greece. These building blocks of Neoclassicism almost always featured a processional entrance, grand enough to make visitors feel both special and diminutive at the same time. Neoclassical houses built today strive to conjure up the same mixture of emotions, albeit on a much smaller scale.

Pleasing portico
Nelles Manor, in Ontario, Canada, is a Georgian-styled house with a Neoclassical flourish. This portico, or porch, is one example of the latter. With a central barrel vault in its ceiling and slim Hellenistic columns, the porch is not in Georgian character at all but it does make a lovely quirky addition to the façade.

Neoclassical surround

The windows of Neoclassical houses are often remarkably similar to those in Georgian houses. However, they feature slimmer mullions and often include some design flourish at the window head – a small pediment or semicircular Roman arch being the most common.

Doorway fanlight

Neoclassical doorways often feature a semi-elliptical fanlight above the door and slim sidelights to each side of the door. These glazed elements are often framed with the slimmest of mullions, which are often curved to form a sculptural contrast to the rigour of the symmetry and form of the architecture.

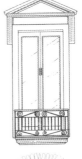

Decorative surround

Both door and window frames often featured some form of decorative surround. This was not a grand gesture but more a tasteful quirk, usually in the form of a painted wooden or stone pilaster and cornice. The colour of these adornments was almost invariably white when paired with brickwork, or neutral when used with stone.

Pedimented porch

Even a small house can include Classical architecture, as shown by this porch with a pediment. When well executed, such flourishes can add to the design of any house. However, when mismatched or overemphasised, Classical can quickly turn to catastrophe.

Ornamentation

Portico detailing
Rose Hill Manor, in
Frederick County,
Maryland, features a
double-storey portico.
One of the unusual
aspects of its design is
the use of two different
types of columns – the
lower ones being Doric
(see their plain capitals),
while the scrolled upper
ones are Ionic.

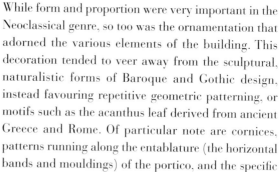

While form and proportion were very important in the
Neoclassical genre, so too was the ornamentation that
adorned the various elements of the building. This
decoration tended to veer away from the sculptural,
naturalistic forms of Baroque and Gothic design,
instead favouring repetitive geometric patterning, or
motifs such as the acanthus leaf derived from ancient
Greece and Rome. Of particular note are cornices,
patterns running along the entablature (the horizontal
bands and mouldings) of the portico, and the specific
design of the capitals on
the top of columns, each
telling of a different
Classical order. Also, look
out for any detailing
within the central portion
of the pediment, which
will generally be a frieze
with figures depicting a
scene from ancient times.

Corinthian column

Ionic column

Ornate cornice

This ornamental detail exemplifies the thought that went into the proportion of every element of Neoclassical design – and the craftsmanship required for its execution. The cornice embodies several classical motifs: the fret, the egg and dart, the bead and fillet and the honeysuckle.

Column capitals

Capitals are the top portion of columns and although they can be finished in any shape most adhere to one of the five Classical orders – Ionic, Composite, Doric, Tuscan and Corinthian. In Renaissance times these orders were rediscovered and have been a major influence in architecture ever since.

Pilasters

Pilasters are decorative versions of columns that are picked out in relief on the main wall. They have no structural purpose but serve to add interest to the façade, door or window surround and are therefore often used in conjunction with real columns, often supporting a frieze or fake entablature.

Balustraded cupola

Balustrades are used extensively on Neoclassical houses as guard rails on balconies, around the edge of a shallow-pitched roof, in front of an ornamental window and even bordering a cupola. Their shape is often a form of bulbous urn, a reference taken from ancient Roman architecture.

Interior Design

Overt decoration

The dining room in Vanderbilt Marble House in Newport, Rhode Island, has almost too much for the eye to focus on. The walls are adorned with plasterwork, which forms frames inside which pictures have been painted; pilasters border the fireplace and the polished table completes a room of the utmost opulence.

Just as architects took their lead from ancient Greek and Roman structures, so the interior design of houses was also based upon these age-old ideals. Pilasters feature heavily, as door or fireplace surrounds, panel-making devices on walls and vertical borders to openings. Cornices are heavy and Classically influenced, while frescos and sculptural bas-reliefs also depict scenes from ancient times and are framed in panels. Neoclassical interior design is 'high design', decoration for the fabulously wealthy, and thus is not often seen anywhere but in the most prestigious of historic homes.

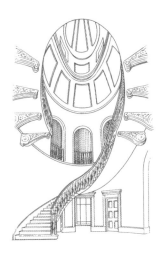

Grand staircase
Elizabeth Bay House, in Sydney, Australia, was designed by English architect John Verge. The extravagantly sweeping, curved staircase is a prime example of the Neoclassical tendencies of Regency architecture of the time. Notice also the scrolled supports to the landing and the arches leading off from the upper floor.

Scrolls and ox heads
Plasterwork was a major element in the interior decoration of Neoclassical houses and elaborate detailing such as scrollwork and even bucrania (stylised ox head motifs) were often incorporated.

Roman arches
Two predominant arch types were used in Neoclassical design – the flattened semi-elliptical arch and, more importantly, the Roman arch. This most simple semi-circular arch was taken from ancient Rome and has stood the test of time, while other more elaborate arches – such as the pointed Gothic arch – have been largely unused since their popularity declined.

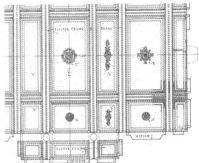

Ceiling detail
Panelling was not restricted to walls. Here, intricate plasterwork is used to create the effect of panels, while rosettes are applied to the centre of some panels. Note how the panels get smaller towards the periphery.

Introduction

Australian dynasty

A famous Sydney landmark, Caerleon is a Victorian house with a lot of history. Its design recalls English houses of the same era, apart from additions such as the veranda at ground level and walk-out balcony above the bay window. These are antipodean touches.

In Victorian architecture, as in Georgian and Edwardian, a style prevailed rather than a specific design type. Victorian style is so named because it coincides with the reign of Queen Victoria (1837–1901) but within it are various subgenres such as Queen Anne, Jacobethan, Italianate and Gothic Revival. However, what these styles tend to have in common is a reaction against the symmetrical designs associated with Palladian and Georgian buildings. Architects embraced advances in material technology, using steel within their designs, and freely mixed and matched styles, incorporating Gothic elements such as pointed arches into buildings with steep Tudoresque roofs, for example.

Victorian architecture permeated the British Empire and Australia was no exception. Built in 1885, Caerleon is an historic house in Sydney, designed by architect Harry Kent for Charles B. Fairfax. Victorian traits such as bay windows, gables with a 45-degree pitch and stone-dressed red brick walls are supplemented with leaded glass windows and a wrought-iron veranda, elements that point to the Queen Anne style, which became so popular in Australia around the late 19th century.

Victorian house design spread rapidly throughout the world. The architectural style is an adaptable one, its identifying elements being many and interchangeable, making it easy to incorporate in almost any size and type of house. Additionally, the way in which architects dispensed with the constraints of the more formal genres that had gone before appealed to the general public and Victorian house design became almost universal in its popularity.

An example of this popularity can be seen in San Francisco, where tens of thousands of Victorian houses were built between the middle and late 19th century. Whereas British architects largely stuck to the ideal of red brick with white stone dressing, in San Francisco designers painted the exterior of houses, picking out the architectural details in white and filling in the panels, usually in three or more bright colours. The effect was, and still is, loved and hated in equal measure by architecture buffs but, liked or not, it has become famous and given rise to the term 'Painted Ladies'.

Painted Ladies
Painting the façade accentuates the extravagant detailing of Victorian design. Notice the timberwork at cornice level as well as the decorative stucco in panels. These San Francisco houses have become gaudy sculptures; reminders of a joyful period in residential architectural history.

Archetypes

English Victorian

Red brick, terracotta shingles and a carved stone porch are just three of the traits that mark out this house as a typical Victorian design. That said, 'typical' is a difficult word to use for Victorian design because the houses are so varied in shape and decoration – another defining characteristic of the style.

While American architects designed timber-clad Victorian houses and painted their exteriors in bright colours, their English counterparts were content to design in the reds and browns of brick and terracotta, interspersed with white stone detailing. This London house for English illustrator, Kate Greenaway, was designed by Richard Norman Shaw. A playful lack of symmetry (unheard of in previous styles) is evident in the form and detailing, while the bay window, large chimney and prominent mid-pitched gable all shout out that this is a Victorian design.

Victorian Gothic

The Victorian era encompassed a variety of different styles including Gothic Revival. This period dwelling features a particularly steeply pitched gable roof, a pointed arch design to the decorative bargeboard and a conical tower. The design is extravagant but at the same time not over the top – a good example of Victorian architecture.

English cottage

The one-and-a-half-storey cottage-style house was popular in rural England and Victorian design only enhanced the quaint beauty of the genre. In this particular case, the dormers, gable and porch are all adorned with decorative timberwork, while the small bay window on the upper storey has some Neoclassical traits.

English terrace

In Britain the archetypal Victorian house will never be without a bay window. Here, what could be a row of sedate Georgian houses is transformed by the addition of bay windows to the front façade. The bay immediately alters the look of the houses and tells us that they were built in the mid- to late 19th century, rather than a hundred years earlier.

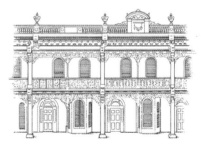

Australian terrace

The warm climate of southern Australia influences house design and, in contrast to the bay-windowed British Victorian terrace, this one in Melbourne features balconies with wonderfully ornate wrought-iron balustrades. The urns on the rooftop balustrade recall Classical styles and are in keeping with the arched Romanesque-inspired windows of the properties.

Archetypes

Carson Mansion

If it were in Disneyland, a princess would live here but in fact this house (now a hotel) is a classic example of the extravagances that American architects brought to the Queen Anne style in the Victorian era.

Victorian design transcends rigid ideas about form or the use of particular materials. Instead, it is a collaboration of styles and architectural ideals which culminate in a delightful hotch-potch of immediately accessible built forms, which have endured more than a hundred years of additions and alterations. Here, the meticulously maintained Carson Mansion, the former home, in Eureka, California, of timber baron William Carson has exaggerated every decorative element and feature. Thankfully most Victorian houses were less ostentatious.

Italianate style

Perhaps the most formally decorative Victorian style is Italianate architecture. Harking back to Italian Renaissance design, houses such as this one sprang up across the USA during the mid-19th century. Their designs were made possible by new materials – metal – and mass production, which made them more widely affordable.

American adaptation

The Orin Jordan House, built by Orin Jordan in 1888, makes use of asymmetrical Victorian design to incorporate a variety of verandas and screen rooms, which make it more suitable to the warm climate of Whittier, California. On a Georgian house these additions could well look out of place but here they are perfectly suited.

South African quirks

Diminutive but decorative, this Victorian bungalow in South Africa is a fine example of the use of a red and white colour scheme in this period of house. The white-striped façade to the bay window complements the painted sculptural stonework, while a jaunty Gothic-style roof feature adds distinction to this otherwise low-slung building.

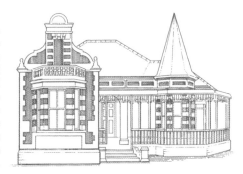

Sagamore Hill (1884)

Presidential Victoriana
Designed by architects
Lamb & Rich, Sagamore
Hill is not the most
extravagant Victorian
(Queen Anne) style
house in the USA but it
was fit for a president.
Roosevelt was renowned
for his exuberant
personality, which this
house fits perfectly.
He lived here until his
death in 1919.

This grand Queen Anne-style mansion in Long Island, New York, was the home of President Theodore Roosevelt between 1885 and 1919. Sagamore Hill, as it is named, is now a National Historic Site and also home to the Theodore Roosevelt Museum (in a separate building). The house itself has been preserved, its multitude of gables, dormers and pedimented porches creating a striking design bearing all the hallmarks of Victorian architecture without being overly extravagant. As with most Victorian houses, the architecture has been allowed to flow with no symmetrical restraint and so feels far more organic than Georgian houses of the same stature. Internally, the same is true and it seems that Sagamore Hill must have been a wonderfully interesting place to live.

Main gable, south elevation

The enormous main gable of Sagamore Hill's south elevation is home to a group of four sash windows, set side by side, with a frieze between the centre two. The decorative aspect of this element is at odds with the rest of the house but serves as a focal point for the massive gable, so minimising some of the monumentality of the structure.

Trophy room

The trophy room in Sagamore Hill is a big-game hunter's paradise. It is also a great example of Victorian extravagance: the vaulted ceiling heightening the room's importance, while decorative columns and pilasters support a heavily sculpted cornice. With typical Victorian confidence, no area of wall space is left unfilled, be that with a buffalo head or painting.

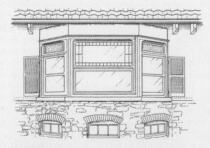

Library window

The library bay window features an especially wide central sash with beautifully detailed leaded glass and curved corners to the frame head. Fluting to the wooden frame is an example of the attention to detail and decoration so often found on Victorian dwellings, even those of less importance than a president's home.

Chimney stacks

The multiple chimneys of Sagamore Hill are a testament to the house's size. The design of the chimney stacks is another indication of Victorian designers' penchant for decoration. The brickwork of the stacks is precise and detailing is noticeable without being overly extravagant, a feature of the overall architectural design of the house.

Materials & Construction

Classic form
Tinakilly House in County Wicklow, Ireland, is, unusually for a Victorian house, quite symmetrical in design. However, the architect's bay-window design is very Victorian. The use of a thick stone wall with a grey mortar render was also typical of Victorian properties in Ireland in the late 19th century.

Victorian houses use many different materials and assume an assortment of forms, depending upon their designer and their location. However, as can be seen here, at Tinakilly House, they are almost always easily recognisable. The house's double bay windows, ornamental chimneys and central front entrance display its Victorian credentials well. Completed in 1883, after taking ten years to build, Tinakilly was the home of industrialist Captain Robert Halpin. It was designed for him by James Franklin Fuller and the duo worked on the plans that specified brick for the basement but a stone and mortar upper structure.

Australian veranda

Yallum Park is one of the best preserved Victorian houses in Australia. Its veranda is not unusual in the country and is a design quirk that Australian architects included on houses of the period, adapting them from their English origins to better serve home owners in the hot southern Australian climate.

Contrasting coloured brickwork

Victorian houses have many decorative features but one of the most noticeable (and easiest to achieve) was contrasting colours in the materials used to build the house. Whether created in different types of bricks or white painted elements of light-coloured stone next to red brickwork, the contrast always shouted 'Victorian'.

English terrace design

The archetypal design of an English Victorian terrace was what is known as 'two up, two down' – a description of the main rooms in the house. Often the house extended at the rear to offer another bedroom and a scullery with access to a small backyard, which was often shared with neighbours.

Doors & Windows

Tricky traits

Max Gate was built during the Victorian age but it has numerous design quirks that come from earlier eras. For example, the small-paned windows are more akin to Georgian design. Most Victorian houses favoured larger panes of glass with fewer elements within each sash window.

The penchant of Victorian designers for bay windows has already been mentioned – they are the single most recognisable defining element of Victorian architecture. However, there are other features that should also be considered, including certain nuances that offer more subtle clues about the architectural heritage of a house. Max Gate, the Dorset home that English novelist Thomas Hardy designed and his brother built, has some unusual features and no bay window, but the pointed head of its entrance porch is a good indication of its genre, as are the hipped-roofed towers and large gable on the roof.

Bay windows and balustrades

Italianate in design, this Australian house has the hallmark large bay window (with the added touch of balustrading above) of a Victorian-era house. The thick sculpted pillars between the windows add to the drama of the design, making this a great example of the showmanship of the Victorian period.

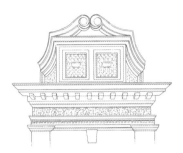

Ornate porch detail

Why have a normal porch when you can have an ornate cornice, complete with a scroll-topped mini bay window above, too? This type of intricately designed porch head detail is not uncommon on houses built in the mid- to late 19th century. The entrance to the home was considered important in Victorian houses as this style of adornment demonstrates.

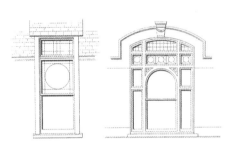

Sash window and surround

While Victorian designers liked to use larger panes of glass in their sash windows, they were not above including small glazed elements if it meant being able to add decoration to a window. Often, the top sash featured leaded glass designs, many of which had coloured glass.

Door lantern

A glass lantern, originally a surround for a candle or oil-burning wick, can often be spotted installed above the front door of a Victorian mansion. This one, at Carlyle's House in Chelsea, London, is a simple yet functional design that would have lit the doorstep below more than adequately.

Ornamentation

Victorian architecture was a reaction to the staid formality of its predecessors. Instead of symmetry and minimal adornment, Victorian architects gloried in unusual, overly accentuated stylings. They stuck sculptures on parapets, used contrasting colours, and emphasised quirks in form. Then there was Antoni Gaudí. At his most prolific in the Victorian era, Gaudí had a style all of his own. However, the curves, patterns and spires of his unusual buildings did sit within the new Victorian spirit of decoration. While unique in form Casa Milà, a Barcelona apartment block, alludes to more conventional bay windows and its chimneys are high and proud like many Victorian houses of the day.

A Victorian oddity

Casa Milà, in Barcelona, Spain, is quite unique. Designed by Antoni Gaudí, it rides roughshod over any architectural dictat previous laid down. But, while it cannot be put into a single genre, the building exemplifies the excitement in architecture during the Victorian period and represents architectural creativity at its finest.

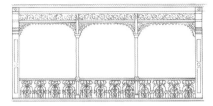

Australian filigree

The veranda fronting a house in Essendon, Victoria, Australia provides a key example of the filigree style so loved by antipodean Victorian architects. The amazing intricacy of the wrought-iron balustrade and veranda frames matches the decorative nature of the cornice and parapet.

Gingerbread

Gingerbread is an American term coined to describe pretty detailing applied to house eaves, balconies and verandas. While similar to Australian filigree, the American version was more commonly created from wood and involved all manner of twists and scrolls, some with quite a Gothic influence.

Round towers

What could be more grand, or indeed more ridiculous, than a tower protruding from one corner of a house? Useless in terms of adding space to a house, but a sure way of attracting attention, towers such as this were a favourite of Victorian architects, especially those influenced by Gothic architecture.

Victorian

While this house has steep gables, as might be seen in Gothic design, the windows have flatter headstones (in this case eyebrow lintels) and there is also a bay window. These traits point to a Victorian design – a theory backed up by the patterning in the brickwork and stained glass above the front door.

Interior Design

Period glamour
Designed in the Gothic Revival style, Roseland Cottage, by Joseph C. Wells, features many pointed arch windows with coloured leaded lights. In particular, the conservatory has a large Gothic-style window made up of five smaller pointed arches with coloured glass panels above. The effect is stunning and one not often seen until the Victorian period.

Victorian houses are just as lavishly styled inside as they are on the exterior. The carpentry is often detailed, with trim (architraves and skirting) featuring an assortment of intricate profiles. The windows have coloured panes and the doors feature raised or inset panels. Influences such as Gothic or Renaissance design were often carried through to the interior, with arches and cornices framing entrances and rooms in period splendour. At Roseland Cottage in Woodstock, Connecticut, built for the Bowen family in 1846, the interior is a riot of extravagant wall and floor coverings and dappled coloured light, shining in through windows resplendent with yellow, red, purple and blue glazed pieces.

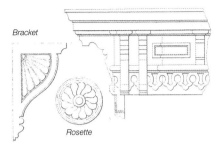

Bracket

Rosette

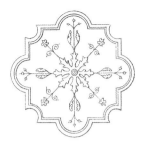

Extravagant cornices

Taking reference from Renaissance design, Victorian architects and interior designers often added a cornice to finish the junction between wall and ceiling. These moulded decorative elements were almost universally oversized and extremely detailed in their mould profile.

Ceiling rose

How best to set off that crystal chandelier in the centre of the parlour? A ceiling rose was the way to go in Victorian times. Moulded from plaster, in the same technique used to make cornices, these decorative mouldings were often large and extravagant, creating a fitting centrepiece for the ceiling and room.

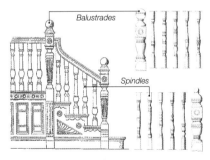

Balustrades

Spindles

Mosaic floor tiling

Terracotta and ceramic tiling came very much into fashion in Victorian times. In the UK, terracotta shingles were often used on the exterior of buildings. Internally, mosaics could be found, most commonly adorning the floors and lower portions of walls in entrance halls.

Staircase spindles and turned balusters

Turned wooden balustrades featuring many slim spindles were the norm for staircases in Victorian houses. Turned balusters with curvaceous and often bulbous portions were common; their inspiration came from Queen Anne design, an influential style used by architects throughout the Victorian era.

Introduction

Arts and Crafts, US style

The design of the Gamble House, built in 1908 by Charles and Henry Greene using traditional timber building techniques, glorifies the materials and methods used. Surrounding walkways and walls are hewn from local stones and every detail is crafted using age-old techniques. The result is an honest architecture that aims to champion the artisan and the traditional techniques used in its construction.

The Arts and Crafts movement began as a reaction to the seemingly ever-decreasing importance given to the decorative arts and traditional artisans in the face of the progressive industrialisation of society. The movement's proponents championed traditional craftsmanship and old, even medieval styles of work and decoration. Their ideas flourished between 1860 and the first decade of the 1900s.

The movement began in the UK but soon spread to northern Europe and the United States. Its instigator is purported to be artist and writer William Morris and his ideals were quickly espoused by a variety of architects, designers and artists. In America, the movement is often referred to as American Craftsman or simply Craftsman style and examples of its architecture are exemplified in houses such as the Gamble House in Pasadena, California.

The style of Arts and Crafts houses was uniquely dependent upon their location due to the fact that local craftspeople always tended to work with the materials most readily available to them. While this was done with other styles, often in order to add local charm, with Arts and Crafts it was a prerequisite of the movement and so houses built in the UK were very different from their American counterparts even though they were designed by Arts and Crafts architects.

A fine example of an English Arts and Crafts home is The Barn, a house built in 1896 in Exmouth, Devon. Designed by Edward Schroeder Prior, the building's load-bearing structure is a cavity wall, using a brick inner skin but an outer one of red sandstone and beach pebbles, embedded in concrete. The result is a wonderfully textured surface that complemented the original thatched roof very well. Crowning the design are two stone-clad chimney stacks. Cylindrical in form, these are very rustic in appearance. Other elements, such as the windows and doors, are robust, their heavy frames an indication of the movement's traditional ideals, while also working well with the weighty appearance of the stone-clad walls.

Arts and Crafts, UK style
Differing immensely from its American Arts and Crafts counterparts (see facing page), this English house is nonetheless of the same genre. The use of local materials and traditional crafts means stone walls and thatched roofs, plus a wonderfully asymmetric design.

Archetypes

Adirondack style
No other style is so
in tune with nature
and materials as the
Adirondack buildings
in New York State.
Taking local logs and
stones, and introducing
branches into the
stickwork railing and
leaf motifs (see the
bargeboards), this
boathouse with
accommodation above
combines rustic and
crafted elements perfectly.

Tradition is a very important aspect of Arts and Crafts architecture, so much so that designers often borrowed from previous architectural genres, especially those which were prevalent before the rise of High Architecture (the designs of the 18th century, often associated with the Renaissance). In the case of the great Adirondack houses, designers took reference both from their forefathers – being inspired by early settlers' log cabins – but also from nature. These often huge mansions used a proliferation of timber in their construction, all beautifully worked by skilled craftsmen. The effect was rustic yet extremely grand – the perfect mix of exquisite craft and artistic understatement.

Chalet style

Taking inspiration from the archetypal Swiss chalet, this Canadian house, designed by Samuel Maclure in 1900, features an over-sailing roof and a large balcony over the main entrance. The contrasting coloured window frames and robust balustrade on the balcony are clear statements of the house's Arts and Crafts heritage.

Revival style (right)

With a combination of stone and wattle and daub walls, this English Arts and Crafts house is greatly influenced by the Tudor style developed over 400 years prior to its construction. The tall chimney stacks are too slender for a Tudor house, however. Here, the architect has afforded advances in craft a chance to shine, showing just what a skilled brickworker can do.

Half-timbered

The Edzell Mansion, in Toorak, Melbourne, Australia, is a fine example of a late-19th century house that takes inspiration from the half-timbered designs of the Tudor period. Designed by Reed, Smart & Tappin, the use of herringbone red brick between timbers is unusual for the area.

Archetypes

Four square

The square shape of this Wisconsin house tells us that it is a four square. Couple that with the Craftsman-style carpentry work and the rusticated stone pillars that support the veranda, this house is a great example of how Arts and Crafts architecture was a style perfectly suited to semi-urban lots.

American architects of the late 19th and early 20th centuries reacted to the highly decorated and overly designed Victorian houses that had gone before by creating a new house type for the masses: the four square. Fitting right into the Arts and Crafts movement that was sweeping the United States, these large, simply designed houses featured four square rooms on each of their two main levels. The hipped roof often contained another half storey. Detailing was minimal but craftsmanship and construction was of good quality, a trait that marked these new houses out as Arts and Crafts.

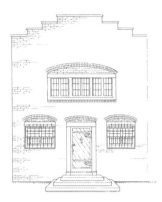

Brick built

Located in Washington, DC, the Edward Lind Morse Studio is an unusual but interesting example of how Arts and Crafts architecture in the United States could mean more than rustic timber design. Note the decorative brickwork around the frames and large forged hinges on the front door.

Combination of styles (left)

William McMillan House in Surrey, British Columbia, was built in the latter part of the Arts and Crafts era and it includes a surprising mix of styles. While the overall craftsmanship is Arts and Crafts, the Doric columns that support the porch roof are Classical in their inspiration and the chamfered gables to the roof hint at Tudor Cottage architecture.

Craftsman style in stone

Timber may have been the most common material for American houses during the Arts and Crafts period but some dwellings, such as the Lummis House in California, bucked the trend. Here, large river stones are used to build a striking structure that would take much skill to erect. The house looks Spanish because it is built in an area with a strong South American influence.

The Red House (1859)

Medieval manners

With arched entrances and steeply pitched roofs, the Red House has many features of medieval architecture. The highest level of craftsmanship is evident in every aspect of the design, and the inscription on the fireplace, *Ars Longa, Vita Brevis*, might be an Arts and Crafts mantra – *the life so short, the craft so long to learn.*

Widely regarded as the father of the Arts and Crafts movement, William Morris commissioned his friend Philip Webb to design his house in Bexleyheath, Kent, in 1859. The Red House, as it has become known because of its use of red brick for the exterior at a time when most other houses were clad in stucco, is a glorious example of the ideals of the movement. Its use of local materials and incorporation of so many aspects of traditional crafts – from masonry to glass blowing and interior decoration – can be widely appreciated as the house was acquired by the National Trust in 2003 and is now open to the public.

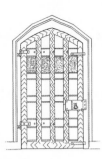

Decorative doors

This striking door has almost too many Arts and Crafts traits to mention. The frame and door head have a double curved, pointed arch. The door itself has multiple panels, coloured glazing and painted patterns, and hand-forged 'T' hinges with traditional studs to secure them. It is a tour de force of Arts and Crafts design.

Ceiling of drawing room

The drawing room was a light-filled space in which Morris often spent time. Its clean white walls contrast with the dark wooden details of the vaulted ceiling. This design was totally at odds with the Victorian movement, which was so popular at the time. Instead, it was a clear nod to Tudor interiors of some 400 years earlier.

The well

Built as sturdily as it is cute in appearance, the well in the garden exemplifies the quality of construction that went into the Red House. The brick well walls, red slate-tiled roof and heavy timber frame represent three different crafts in this one small folly.

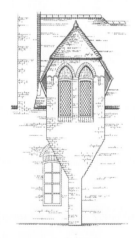

Façade detail

Some windows in the Red House are arched – the pointed arches denoting a Gothic styling – but others are square-headed. However, even these windows include a masonry detail that hints at the pointed arch: a quirky allusion to the past even when the windows are of a more functional aesthetic.

Materials & Construction

Stone and wood
The Riordan Mansion
in Flagstaff, Arizona
was built by brothers
Michael and Timothy
Riordan as a home for
their families in 1904.
The self-builders used
local timber and stone
to construct a rambling
house that today is
considered a quirky
take on the Arts and
Crafts style.

Materials and construction were the driving force
behind the Arts and Crafts movement. The material
and the way it was honed for use by traditional craft
methods were glorified in houses of the era. Whether
built of wood, stone or brick, houses designed in the
Arts and Crafts style displayed the craft used to build
them – wooden rafters protruded at the roof edge,
brickwork was never covered with stucco, even
decorative elements displayed the technique that went
into making them. Arts and Crafts architecture
presented an honesty and traditional allegiance in the
face of an increasingly technological world.

Shingle siding

Shingles are an underused siding material. They are often seen on roofs or as decorative panels on new 'Craftsman' houses but here, on the Isaac Bell House, built in 1881 in Newport, Rhode Island, well-weathered shingles cover most of the external façade.

Timber frame

Post-and-beam construction has long been a tradition across the world due to its sturdy nature and use of local materials. Here, the design is celebrated in a new house, the load-bearing structure of the house being put on display rather than hidden within plaster-clad walls.

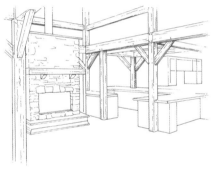

Celebrating stone

Stone is possibly the oldest building material in the world and here it is used to great effect, in pieces large and small, to build an Arts and Crafts-style house.

Note the combination of large mason-worked boulders to the pillars and chimney stack, plus small inset river stone on the main façade.

Doors & Windows

Unusual windows

The Hohenhof in Hagen, Germany, is striking for many reasons, but the variety of window designs stands out. With its 'eyebrow' windows in the roof, bay windows with unusual small lower glazed panels, and rows of rectangular windows with wrought-iron grills in front, the overall effect is quite magical.

While elements such as doors and windows are taken for granted in much new architecture, they offered a chance for a skilled carpenter to show off his trade during the Arts and Crafts era. Both form and detailing (traditional joints and hand-crafted decorations) were glorified. Windows and doors often had arched heads and multiple mullions or panels. Even the hinges that operated doors and windows were specially made, being beaten or cast by blacksmiths and metalworkers into artistic forms that suited the wonderfully constructed pieces that they hung.

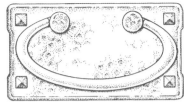

Architects continue to look to the Arts and Crafts movement for inspiration. For example, ironmongers still produce hardware for doors that harks back to the period. The door knocker and handle shown here are brand new but could well have been made by a blacksmith in the late 19th or early 20th centuries, such is the design and influence from the era.

Coloured glazing

The manufacture of leaded windows was quite an art and one that the Arts and Crafts movement often championed. Skilled glaziers used coloured glass to create stunning picture panels for doors and windows, such as this one at Bramall Hall in Stockport, Cheshire.

Window detail

The Fleur de Lys Studios, in Providence, Rhode Island, were designed by Sydney Burleigh and Edmund Wilson. The many windows on the front façade reference Tudor glazing – their leaded lights made up of a multitude of small panes. Note also the protruding triangular bay windows of the upper floor.

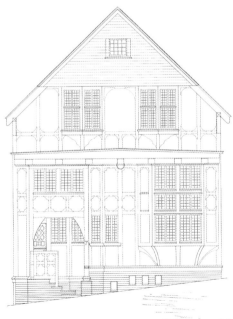

Ornamentation

The ultimate bungalow
Designed by renowned
architects Greene &
Greene, Thorsen House
in Berkeley, California,
is the ultimate bungalow.
Its low-slung appearance
and extensive use of
wood draws inspiration
from the rustic cabins
of America's original
settlers. Leaded glass
panels with natural
designs add to the
Arts and Crafts aura
of the house.

Ornamentation was not something that Arts and Crafts proponents advocated purely on aesthetic grounds. This genre's architects and builders adorned their houses in order to glorify construction techniques and built with extraordinary care and skill according to often ancient techniques. The results of their work can be seen on many houses today. Where modern houses tend to hide the structure and materials of which they are built, Arts and Crafts houses positively glow with it. Of particular note are exposed rafters, rusticated stonework, decorative brick patterns, ironwork on doors and windows, panelled shutters, but there are many other beautifully crafted built elements.

Rustic piers and columns

Stone piers and columns are a favourite of the Arts and Crafts movement. Often using rough hewn stones, the piers create great contrast to the main walls of this Australian house, while complementing the massive stone window surrounds. To add a quirky finish, the columns themselves are Classical in their inspiration.

Half-timber panelling

The Tudor influence is obvious on this house in Pittsburgh, Pennsylvania. The steeply pitched roof and half-timbered façade detail work well on this two- and-a-half-storey town house.

Rafters exposed

This Texan house uses contrasting colours to make a statement of the overhanging roof eaves with their exposed rafter detail. On a different style of house this element would be covered up or designed out, but here it makes an interesting feature that adds to the rustic charm of the house.

Interior Design

Scottish master

Hill House in Glasgow, Scotland, was designed by Arts and Crafts architect Charles Rennie Mackintosh. Renowned not only for his architecture and art but also his distinctive interior and furniture designs, Rennie Mackintosh is often compared to Frank Lloyd Wright for his all-encompassing house designs.

The careful design and construction of the interior of an Arts and Crafts house was just as important to its builder as the outside. Traditional techniques were used to build the internal elements of the house and to decorate it, too. Wood was often a source of inspiration, and furniture and panelling were frequently handmade. The father of Arts and Crafts, William Morris, was renowned for the wallpapers that he produced; their designs taking reference from medieval and naturalistic scenes. There are no specific defining elements to the interior decoration of this genre of house, apart from the fact that everything should look handmade and crafted to perfection.

Warm welcome

The Gamble House in Pasadena, California, offers fine examples of how high-quality carpentry was used to decorate the interior of a home. From the diagonal floorboards to the understated but beautifully finished wall panels and the decorative ceiling beams, wood abounds, creating a rich ambiance full of warmth and character.

Simple staircase

A simple staircase crafted entirely in wood is elevated to a work of some distinction by the care taken with the panelling that runs up its side and the decorative flourish in the form of an extended newel post at the bottom of the balustrade and on the half landing. This is carpentry with extra artistry.

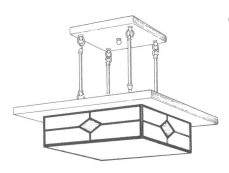

Ornate lighting

This hanging ceiling light fixture is the epitome of the Arts and Crafts movement. The trades required to make it include carpenter, ironworker and glass artist. Combined, their skills produce a stunning piece of craft that is beautiful as much for its manufacture as the design itself.

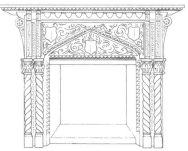

Focal fireplace

Taking wood carving to its highest level, the fire surround at Dimbola Lodge, the Isle of Wight home of photographer Julia Margaret Cameron, is a focal point and an example of how traditional wood crafts could be elevated to the most beautiful elements within an Arts and Crafts house.

Introduction

A new architecture
Designed by William Gray Purcell and George Grant Elmslie, the Purcell-Cutts House in Minneapolis, Minnesota, bears all hallmarks of Prairie-style: flat roofs and bands of windows, the large roof overhangs and central chimney stack. Internally, its layout is open plan, completely disregarding the Victorian ideal of compartmentalised rooms. It is a study in a new American architecture.

The Prairie style, Prairie School or Chicago Group, as this architectural genre and its proponents were variously called, emerged at an interesting point in architectural history. In the late 19th and early 20th centuries, mass production was being promoted as the way forward and yet already the Arts and Crafts Movement was rallying against it. Prairie School architects in the American Midwest sided with their Arts and Crafts counterparts, pushing for handcrafted design and the use of natural materials. However, they also rebelled against the traditionalist architects in America who aspired to Classical Greek and Roman ideals. The Prairie School wanted to create a new style of architecture that was uniquely American.

One of the best-known practices working in the Prairie style at the time was Purcell & Elmslie. Second only to Frank Lloyd Wright in prominence amongst the

Prairie School, the firm designed many houses, including the house for Purcell and his family.

Unlike Victorian or Modernist architecture, the Prairie School was not a movement that influenced architecture worldwide. It was developed by Midwest Americans for their own land and their own people, taking its lead from the prairies themselves. Houses spreading horizontally, their lines accentuating the wide flat expanses of the lands that surrounded the Midwest settlements that had grown into thriving towns.

Dominated by Frank Lloyd Wright, the genre adopted many of his ideologies, for example his belief that Prairie houses should seem as if they had almost grown from their natural surroundings. Taking this tenet further than most, Alfred Caldwell, an often-overlooked master of design, produced numerous structures including pavilions at Eagle Point Park and his own farmhouse in Wisconsin, using natural stone and age-old stone wall construction techniques to create beautifully unique buildings. A landscape architect initially, Caldwell had a gift for creating not just buildings but elements that sat well within the landscape just as Lloyd Wright envisaged.

Prairie meets Modermism

Architect Alfred Caldwell's farmhouse in Bristol, Wisconsin, is a combination of softly rusticated stone walls and glass pavilions that allow the inhabitant (Caldwell himself) to move from inside to out or somewhere in between. It is a convergence of Prairie and the rising trend of Modernism.

Archetypes

Suburban Prairie

John S. van Bergen designed this house for clothing merchant Andrew O. Anderson. Brickwork was favoured by the Prairie School for its textural notes. The living room is dominated by a fireplace occupying an entire wall (a feature favoured by Frank Lloyd Wright). Today, some windows have been replaced and the small panes are out of character. Otherwise the house is a Prairie classic.

The words 'Prairie style' create the impression of some lonesome sprawling ranch built in the middle of vast tracts of uninhabited land. In reality, these homes were more often than not designed for wealthy individuals in the prestigious neighbourhoods of thriving cities. However, unlike many long-colonised European cities, these younger American urban conurbations still had room to grow and land on which these wonderfully horizontal homes could expand. One example is the Andrew O. Anderson House by John S. van Bergen. Built in Dekalb, Illinois, its expansive plan and styling – the low-pitched, hipped roof with large overhangs, banks of windows and stonework detailing – highlight it as a fine example of the Prairie style.

Master and pupil

The Harold C. Bradley House, in Madison, Wisconsin, is attributed in part to the architectural legend Louis Sullivan, along with an upcoming George Elmslie (Purcell & Elmslie). Differing from the low-pitched roofs of other Prairie houses, this home is a delightful crossover from old to new. It embraces the ideals of both architects and still manages to exude a unique American feel and a robust Prairie School aesthetic.

Converging styles

George Maher was an architect apt to do things his own way and the Henry Schultz House, in Winnetka, Illinois, illustrates that perfectly. Here, Maher has combined the English Arts and Crafts aesthetic with that of Prairie architecture. The upright stance of the house and central front door is offset by the low-pitched roof with a large overhang. The effect is unique.

Prairie Modern

Today, Modernist architects, especially those in America, are often influenced by the Prairie School. The flat roofs and concrete structures – so promoted by Modernists – are now tailored into multilayered designs with a horizontal aesthetic that can so easily be traced back to the designs of Frank Lloyd Wright and friends.

Reborn as ranch

Taking Prairie to its limits can mean either the convoluted brilliance of a Frank Lloyd Wright mansion or the stripped-back ideal of a Ranch-style home. Builder Cliff May created many California homes that use the same horizontal, open plan ideals but he forwent the architectural showmanship to produce simple low-slung homes that almost anyone could afford.

Archetypes

Conventional ranch
Evolving from the
Prairie style into the
Ranch style, Midwestern
American homes took on
an even more horizontal
aesthetic. Predominantly
a single storey in height,
these Ranch-style homes
became popular across
the United States, from
Wisconsin to California.

As Prairie School architects got to grips with their genre, they began to understand both the intricacies and adaptabilities of the designs that they were producing. This knowledge brought about new ways of thinking, including potential solutions for low-cost housing. Both Frank Lloyd Wright and John S. van Bergen are credited with designs for inexpensive Prairie-style homes that could have been mass produced, something not envisaged in the original tenets of the genre but, in reality, a natural progression in all housing types from the start of the 20th century onwards. Developers built swathes of these homes on the outskirts of towns and cities, creating the archetypal American suburbia.

Australian Prairie

Considered an original member of the Prairie School, Marion Mahony Griffin was a pioneering female architect from the USA. In 1914, she moved to Australia with her husband, Walter Burley Griffin, and designed this Prairie-influenced home using local materials but sticking to the vertical panelled windows and low-pitched roof lines of her Midwest architectural upbringing.

Modern Prairie (below)

Today, Americans still hanker after the forms and lines of the original Prairie-style homes. This contractor-built house is one of many being built across the United States that draws on what Purcell & Elmslie, Frank Lloyd Wright and contemporaries preached as a new craft-influenced style for the American family.

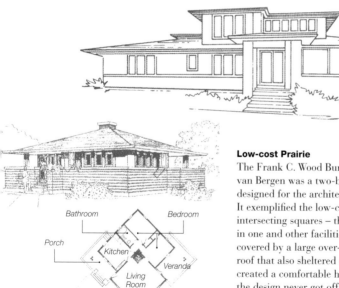

Bathroom

Bedroom

Porch

Kitchen

Veranda

Living Room

Low-cost Prairie

The Frank C. Wood Bungalow by John S. van Bergen was a two-bedroom bungalow designed for the architect's uncle, Frank. It exemplified the low-cost thinking. Two intersecting squares – the main living space in one and other facilities in the other – covered by a large over-sailing low-pitched roof that also sheltered outside deck areas created a comfortable home. Unfortunately, the design never got off the drawing board.

PRAIRIE

Frederick C. Robie House

A design classic
The extremely slim gauge of brick used for the external façade helps to accentuate the linearity of this 1910 home's design. This, along with the stone-topped parapets of the balconies, picked out in a contrasting colour to the brickwork, are examples of how Frank Lloyd Wright used materials to further integrate his ideals into the design of his homes.

Located at 5757 S. Woodlawn Avenue in the Hyde Park district of Chicago, Illinois, the Frederick C. Robie House is perhaps the most famous of Frank Lloyd Wright's Prairie-style homes. Designated a National Historic Landmark in 1963, after several threats of demolition, the house's exaggerated eaves overhangs and its striated front elevation, with three balconies and banks of glazed walls, is the epitome of what Prairie School architects strived to achieve for years to come. Wright did not oversee the construction but entrusted it to Marion Mahony, his first employee. Every aspect of the house, from architecture to furniture, light fittings and tableware, was designed by Wright in order to retain the integrity of the finished work.

South elevation

Looking straight at the south elevation of the Robie House, you can truly appreciate the design's linearity. Even at three storeys high, the building seems to hug the ground, thanks to the number of horizontal lines across the façade – balcony stones, eaves lines, window sills and so forth.

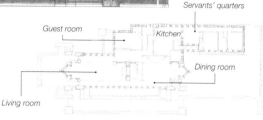

Servants' quarters

Guest room

Kitchen

Dining room

Living room

Second-floor plan

Notice the large expanses of open plan living space, something that we have become accustomed to today but which, at the time of this design, was radically new. Note also the number of window openings; this is a multitude of windows for any house, either in 1910 or today.

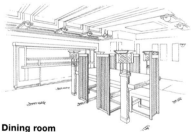

Dining room

The architect designed everything in the house, as well as the structure itself. Here, note the table and chairs, the patterns on the carpet, the dresser integrated into the wall and numerous light fixtures. Few architects went to such lengths and few patrons were accommodating enough to encourage this kind of all-encompassing design.

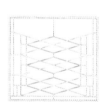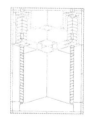

Window detail

Lloyd Wright sometimes took inspiration from nature for his 'Art Glass' window designs but, as here, his usual preference was for geometric patterns. The detailing is extensive and the use of coloured glass adds to the drama of these designs. In all there were 174 decorative glazed panels in 29 different designs in the Robie House.

Materials & Construction

Baronial Prairie

Fair Lane is a grand home, big enough to carry off the turrets on its roofline. This addition is unusual for the Prairie style, but architects of the genre were not averse to using motifs from the past and visually this house does not suffer from a certain amount of extravagant architectural handiwork.

The Prairie School was akin to the Arts and Crafts movement that spread from Europe in that it championed well-crafted designs that often used historic artisanal techniques such as masonry and carving. However, the Americans were not against incorporating new materials such as steel beams to enable truly spectacular home designs. This combination makes the genre a versatile and intriguing part of American architectural history because it combines the old and the new to the best effect. One fine example is Fair Lane, the home of automobile tycoon Henry Ford in Dearborn, Michigan. Built in 1909 the house was originally designed by Frank Lloyd Wright. However, he left to travel Europe and it was completed by Marion Mahony Griffin. Wright then returned, dismissed her and added a number of baronial flourishes.

Brick/stone combination

Contrasting materials, whether light and dark or smooth and rough, give definition to a home design and the Prairie School architects used this to their advantage. So often we see a dark textured brickwork paired with smooth, white stone balustrade cappings and window sills. This accentuates the horizontal nature by adding exaggerated white lines that flow across the façade.

Low-pitched roof

While Tudor houses were renowned for steeply pitched roofs, Prairie houses almost all feature low-pitched, hipped roofs with wide overhangs. Aesthetically, they add to the low-slung design style. Functionally, the large overhang shades the many windows, keeping these houses cool in the summer.

Suppressed chimney

Central to many Prairie-style homes is the fireplace – used both as a heating device and focal point for the main living space. However, it is its design with respect to the external façade that is really interesting. Built large and strong, almost always rectangular in plan, the chimney is squashed down so that there is no interruption of the horizontal design. The result is a squat but powerful nod to verticality amidst many opposing lines.

Doors & Windows

In the band

The windows of the William E. Martin House, in Oak Park, Chicago (designed by Frank Lloyd Wright in 1903), are characteristic of many Prairie-style houses. Deliberately located in bands running around the exterior, they accentuate the horizontality given to the house by its series of low-pitched roofs.

Much like the Arts and Crafts movement, Prairie School architects treasured the techniques and crafts of years gone by. However, their design ethic was not so much about recreating these crafts as using them in new and innovative ways. Doors and windows were treated as decorative pieces within the house designs and, apart from some rare cases where naturalistic designs were incorporated, Prairie architects favoured symmetrical patterns and shapes that could be reproduced in glasswork or machined timber. Influences were taken from Japanese art and design as well as some Art Deco styling. The effect was to provide a magical contrast to the linearity of the houses themselves.

Clerestory windows

These smaller windows positioned above eye level are a great way of allowing more light into a room. They can be incorporated within the main window frame – like an extra window pane added on top – or be a separate entity altogether, as here above the main door. Prairie School architects liked them both for their functionality and as an added decorative element.

Geometric decorative glazing

Leaded window lights and coloured glazing played a major role in bringing art into the Prairie-style house. Called 'art glass' by its proponents, the  stylised designs favoured by the genre tended towards symmetry and geometry – decorative but nothing too fancy that might clash with the carefully conceived horizontality of the building design.

Internal door frames

The carpenter, cabinetmaker or millworker – the name given depending upon where you come from – was a very important tradesperson in Prairie-style houses. Not only was bespoke furniture made for each house but window and door frames were crafted with exquisite care to form part of the overall artistic statement that the house represented.

Front door with fanlights

The fanlight is an architectural quirk used in numerous genres, predominantly Georgian, to bring extra light into the hallway. Fanlights also enabled Prairie architects to show off their 'art glass' design skills over an array of windows. Designs would often encompass the glazed door panels plus a triptych of side and overhead fanlights.

PRAIRIE Ornamentation

Painting Prairie style

The Stockman House is a museum built from Frank Lloyd Wright's 1905 plans for a fireproof house. The recreation of these designs has been carried out with the greatest care and skill. Note that the white stucco finish is contrasted by plum-coloured eaves and rectangular panels to the main façade – a simple but striking colour scheme.

Ornamentation to the Prairie School meant many things but it almost always implied order and symmetrical styling. From the 'art glass' in doors and window frames to sculptures such as urns or stylised figures sitting neatly at either end of a balcony parapet, the design was always balanced. This regimentality did not stifle the architects though and they indulged in decoration, both two- and three-dimensional, to bring their homes to life inside and out. The level of ornamentation used was often determined by the client's purse strings but even the most modest houses (the example here is the Stockman House in Mason City, Iowa) were decorated intelligently.

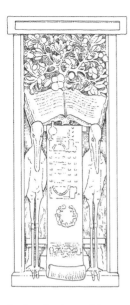

Symmetrical balconies

The balcony is an integral part of many Prairie School houses and it is used as much to exaggerate the horizontal lines of the home as to create extra outdoor space. In this capacity it can be seen as ornamentation – a structural element added for effect – and architects of Prairie influence and beyond still use it like this today.

Sculpted columns (above)

At Frank Lloyd Wright's original home in Oak Park, Chicago, his study is guarded by four columns adorned with rather unusual pilasters. Sculpted for him by Richard W. Bock, the pilasters are decorated with a frieze that features a book, signifying knowledge, two storks for fertility, and an architectural engraving, to illustrate the owner's creativity.

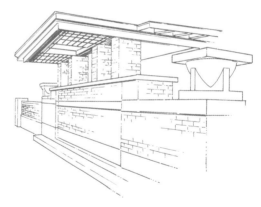

Ornamental flourish

While the overriding motif of Prairie-style homes is the shallow pitch of their roofs, ornamentation such as this lattice-roofed porch or the stone urns that adorn the low balcony walls were common. Quirky additions such as these broke up the architectural rigour of the design and added character.

Interior Design

Open-plan layout
Until the early 1900s, rooms were usually compartmentalised and separate. Prairie School architects turned this on its head with designs that opened up the interior (shown here is the Ralph Baker House in Wilmette, Illinois), creating open plan layouts that blurred the distinction between living and dining space.

No other architectural genre has paid so much attention to the internal design of a home as the Prairie School. While Renaissance interiors were grand, they were often an afterthought or a project undertaken by a separate designer. Prairie architects, led by Frank Lloyd Wright, took it upon themselves to design practically every aspect of the internal design from fireplace to finger bowls, dining table to light fixtures. The result is a series of remarkable spaces that are unbelievably architecturally rich, but often seem devoid of the usual homely accoutrements that owners and time bring to a house.

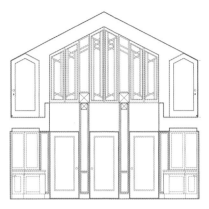

Grandiose design

The Cooley House, Monroe, Louisiana, by Marion Mahony and her husband Walter Burley Griffin is a fine example of Prairie School interior design at its most grand. The end wall of the double-height room is filled with decorated windows. The room is bordered by balconies, giving it more of the feel of a church than a living room.

Architect-designed furniture

To complement the exacting geometric designs so often seen in Prairie School houses, their architects would also design the furniture. Designs ranged from the playful to the austere but most were geometric in style and crafted out of timber and metal. Built-in seating areas in walls and along window edges marked special views or focal points for the occupants.

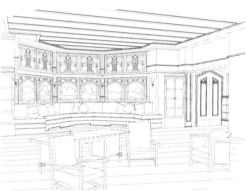

Wooden staircase details

The staircases of these beautifully planned houses would echo the overall design. Neat recessed panels in the newel posts and balustrade columns added an artistry while remaining in keeping with the geometric design. Balusters themselves were often square-cut timber or thin metal railings.

Introduction

The birth of Modernist architecture was the result of a rapidly changing world at the beginning of the 20th century. New materials, such as plate glass, steel and concrete, were beginning to be used in construction and new ideals about what the public expected of their homes, workplaces and leisure spaces were being formed by a group of European architects, whose sights were set on changing the way we lived.

In America, Frank Lloyd Wright and his contemporaries were also altering our perceptions of house construction and although it is Prairie School in style, Lloyd Wright's Robie House (see page 190) is considered a Modern masterpiece due to its use of structural steel beams and its radical open-plan layout.

While recognising Lloyd Wright's brilliance, European architects didn't take to the Prairie style. Instead, they began to develop a new genre in which building form was expressed through its function, and materials were celebrated rather than covered and decorated. Famous Swiss architect Le Corbusier described his designs as 'machines for living', summing up the new way in which architects were thinking about houses and how they should be designed to best service their occupants.

A new way of living
The Masters' Houses, designed as part of the Bauhaus campus in Dessau, Germany, by Walter Gropius, were an enclave of homes for college masters. Conforming to a strict code, the houses' white façades, thin black metal-framed windows and blocky design are the cornerstones of what you will recognise today as Modernist houses.

Different strokes

Amidst the tree-lined avenues of northwest London sits an unusual terrace that looks unlike any of its period-styled neighbours. Built in 1938, the houses numbered 1–3 Willow Road in Hampstead were designed by Erno Goldfinger. From the concrete columns to the elongated rectangular arrangement of windows and crowning flat roof, this was a statement of intent in the heart of a wealthy city suburb.

Gone were the pitched roofs, both steep and shallow. Gone were the decorative pediments on porches and above window heads. Victorian-style bay windows were off limits, as were the Classically inspired columns so beloved of many previous architectural genres. Modernism was, and still is, an exercise in stripping away the pretence of a house design and showing the building for what it is.

A favourite material of Modernists, as much in the early 1900s as today, is concrete. It is strong and easily workable, and, if formed well, its surface can make for striking finishes, whether external or internal. However, other materials – among them steel, glass and wood – are also often used, their properties being championed in designs that step away from the crafted aesthetic of Prairie or Arts and Crafts styling in favour of a more industrial look, a design and finish that one could imagine being created by a machine.

Some people feel that Modernism is inhuman and cold in its ideals. Some have gone on to rally against it and design Postmodern buildings. Others like the clean lines and lack of clutter, and Modernism is the foremost architectural movement in the world today.

MODERNIST **Archetypes**

Clarity of form
Farnsworth House, designed by Ludwig Mies van der Rohe and built near Plano, Illinois, in 1951, is so simple it's see-through. Steel columns support a floor and a roof, and glass walls protect an interior, of which the one element not visible from outside is the bathroom. This is a house distilled to its purest elements.

Modernism began as a bold move into a more technological age and it spawned some great houses and inspired new social housing schemes. It is also responsible for some of the worst mass-housing developments standing today. However, this is the price we pay for architects relearning how to design the house. Out of this melting pot came a distillation of just what Modernism was all about. Certain visionaries such as Le Corbusier, Mies van der Rohe, Louis Kahn and Frank Lloyd Wright worked and reworked their designs to create houses that were the essence of the Modernist ideal.

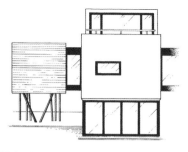

Minimal interpretation

Designed as a series of concrete and wooden boxes, stacked for what architect Francisco J. del Corral del Campo calls a 'programmed space', Stilt House in Granada, Spain, gives occupants both internal and external areas to live in. The box-like aesthetic is almost a disassembly of Gropius' German Masters' Houses (*see page 198*).

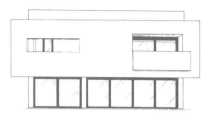

New ideas from old

Built next door to ancient ruins in Korinthos, Greece, this house is a reinterpretation of the Villa Savoye (*see page 6*), a house designed by Le Corbusier and built in France more than 80 years ago. While the design is subtly different, the ideas are the same, showing that the original tenets of Modernism are alive and functioning in the 21st century.

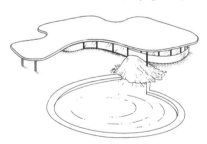

Flowing form

It may have started life as a few lines on a piece of paper but the simplicity and flowing form of Casa das Canoas, the concrete-roofed, glass-walled, single-storey Rio de Janeiro house designed in 1951 by the Brazilian Modernist trail-blazer Oscar Niemeyer, created a building of extraordinary clarity and beauty (*see page 10*).

Postmodernism

While some took to Modernism, others rallied against it. Vanna Venturi House in Philadelphia, Pennsylvania, designed by Robert Venturi for his mother, features a multiple-pitched roof and large broken pediment; there is the allusion to an arch above the entrance, and frivolous ribbed details to the façade. This is Postmodernism – modern but definitely not Modernist.

Archetypes

Simple shapes

The Plus House, in Shizuoka, Japan, by Mount Fuji Architects Studio, neatly illustrates the simple form ideal. The house consists of two rectangular boxes, one stacked on the other and turned at a right angle. This simple pair of boxes makes for an unusual and ultimately stunning design that also fulfils the role of home.

The phrase 'form follows function', attributed to sculptor Horatio Greenough and popularised by architect Louis Sullivan, is a mantra often recited by Modernist architects. It refers to the shape of a building and its form, which should be based upon or evolve from the purpose it is built for. Modernist architecture eschews fanciful flourishes and instead tends to be boxy, the outer form of the building indicating the shape of the rooms within. Of course, this can be interpreted in many ways and as architects continue to explore Modernist ideals so buildings change in shape and style.

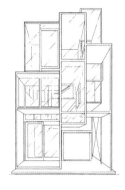

Unique response

As Modernism has progressed, architects have continued to experiment with form and materials. The Clip House in Madrid, Spain, by Bernalte León & Associates, hangs off a massive concrete spinal wall, its living spaces hidden within copper-clad pods with translucent walls. The project takes Modernist ideals and manipulates them to create a new architectural idiom.

Extreme design

Taking the genre to an extreme, House NA, by Sou Fujimoto Architects, is a study in glass and steel. The structure of this Tokyo house is constructed of thin steel beams and its walls are entirely glass. You can observe and appreciate every joint and transition within the building and see exactly how all rooms and functions are connected within.

Experiments in transparency...

Taking an ideal to the extreme has always been the challenge for architects, whether it be bigger, smaller, more decorative or, as in this case, totally transparent. Glass House by Santambrogiomilano, in Milan, Italy, is a house entirely fabricated of glass – its structure and all façades are made of the material, such are the advances in glass technology today.

... or solidity

At first sight, a solid white form, the archetypal house shape, this house in Leiria, Portugal, by Aires Mateus & Associates, plays with our ideas of what a house should be. Its shape looks familiar but once inside the solid block opens up to the sky and extends down into the ground, creating a light-filled home that no one would guess existed from outside.

Neutra House (c. 1940)

A study in closeness
Richard Neutra designed a house of many areas in which occupants could find a solitary space, while opening up the interior to the landscape by extensive use of glass. His philosophy was that access to views of the surrounding countryside made the house itself feel bigger. This blurring of internal and external space is often used today in Modernist houses.

Located at 2300 Silver Lake Boulevard, Los Angeles, California, the home of Richard Neutra – Neutra VDL Studio and Residences – was designed as a study in creating the perfect living space within a confined site. Neutra used natural lighting, great views to the landscape and mirrors as pivotal elements in creating a house that felt much larger than its actual size. The architect said: 'I wanted to demonstrate that human beings, brought together in close proximity, can be accommodated in very satisfying circumstances, taking in that precious amenity called privacy.' He did this with clever design and use of modern materials.

Living room and dining area

Although it is relatively small, the living room and dining area is maximised by Neutra's use of built-in furniture to save space, plus the prodigious number of windows in the room. The resulting light-filled space feels much larger than it would if it were a conventional room with a majority of solid walls.

Penthouse deck

The highest level of the house featured a penthouse suite with a reflecting pool. This shallow pool extends out into the landscape, blurring the boundaries between the house and its surrounding area. It is a simple trick that extends the occupant's ideas of ownership far beyond actual physical boundaries.

Main entrance

The entrance to Neutra's house, via a glazed door under a concrete porch, is unceremonial. Instead, the architect concentrates on flooding the house with natural light, via the double-height glazed façade. Following a fire, louvres were added to this façade to reduce heat gain from the sun.

Materials & Construction

The rise of steel
Structural steel has played a large role in Modernist design since the early 20th century. However, some of the Case Study Houses in Los Angeles took the material to the next level. With steel beams and columns, pressed-steel sheet walls and roofs, houses such as Bailey House, Case Study House 21, had a stripped-down material palette and could be erected very quickly.

Thinking about how a house will affect the lives of its occupants is a Modernist priority and the transition from solidity to transparency forms a major element of this. Furthermore, Modernists believe that functions within the home should be rationalised through design and construction, and that the elements used to build the house should be celebrated in the aesthetic design. With these aspects in mind, Pierre Koenig designed and built Bailey House (Case Study House 21) in Los Angeles in 1959. The simple open-plan layout and almost total transparency are Modernist trademarks. Every aspect of the home's construction is on show: the steel frame, corrugated roof and ceiling beams. This is architecture stripped to its barest essentials, an ideal to which many Modernist architects still aspire today.

Contrast

Casa de Blas, by Alberto Campo Baeza, is a study in the contrast of transparency and solidity. A concrete box punched through with small windows houses the private rooms of this Madrid house, while above a steel-framed glass box serves as a minimalist living room. Light and dark, solid and transparent, concrete and glass: the palette of a Modernist ideal.

Celebrating wood

Wood is often overlooked by Modernists but Molly's Cabin, a holiday home in Georgian Bay, Ontario, by Bing Thom Architects, is a wonderful example of a local material being reinterpreted in a very accessible but obviously Modernist way. The architect has used wood throughout, championing its versatility and weathering qualities in a harsh windswept environment.

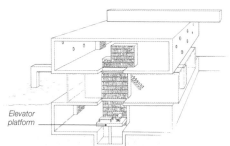

Elevator platform

Building better

Maison à Bordeaux has bedrooms on the lowest level, a glass garden level and an upper level divided into children's and adults' space. The wheelchair-bound occupant has his own 'room', or 'station': the elevator platform. The elevator's movement continuously changes the house's architecture. It is the functional core around which all else is designed.

209

Doors & Windows

Making glass a feature
With a façade almost entirely glass, the Rose Seidler House in Sydney, Australia, is a 1950s example of how Modernist architects, (here Harry Seidler) opened the interior to the landscape. Small opening panes offer ventilation while large windows allow natural light to flood in and provide great views out.

Some extreme Modernist houses are built entirely of glass but most use it more conservatively. While the door merely provides access in and out, the windows offer an opportunity for the Modernist architect to fill the house with light, bring in the landscape, and blur the boundaries between interior and exterior. From the earliest houses of the genre, the view beyond, rather than the frame or surround, has been the salient aspect of a window and architects strive to open up that view, with huge expanses of glass, or to frame it with unusually shaped windows, often located in odd positions on the wall.

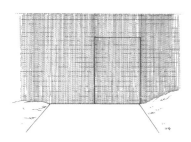

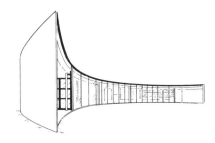

Hidden entrance

A part of the rear façade elevates to reveal the entrance to Sean Godsell's Glenburn House, north of Melbourne, Australia. The doorway is otherwise hidden, disguised within a façade stripped of adornments and so reduced to its purest form and material elements. Enter inside, however, and the house opens up to the landscape beyond via a fully glazed front façade.

Deferring to the view

It is all about the view. Crescent House in Wiltshire, England, by Ken Shuttleworth, is crescent shaped. The hunched outer walls are solid and defensive, offering only one small entry point. However, the concave inner wall of the crescent is entirely glazed. Every room in the house has a view out onto the garden.

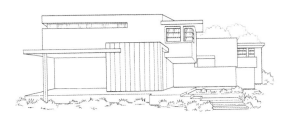

Ribbon window

The classic Modernist window is long and thin, often passing around a corner of the building. The ribbon window is almost always frameless (or with the thinnest, most discreet of metal frames). It has been used since the start of the 20th century, when Walter Gropius designed it into his Bauhaus Masters' Houses, and it continues to be popular today.

Doorways without fanfare

Almost lost within the metal framework of the façade, the door to Charles and Ray Eames' Californian home is a simple continuation of the wall, the only clues to its whereabouts being a small handle and lock. To early Modernists the doorway was not a significant element. Aspects such as transparency and continuation of form and aesthetic were much more important.

Ornamentation

Ornamentation is not something that most Modernists have ever considered unless it arises from the specific functional design of the house. Instead, most Modernist houses find their beauty through the interplay of structural elements and their interaction with their surroundings. By contrast, the Postmodernists actively seek to include decorative flourishes as part of a battle against the 'form follows function' dictat that the majority of Modernist architects have aspired to. Postmodernism is still practised marginally but its popularity was short-lived in the 1970s and 80s, with people quickly falling in and out of love with the irony of it.

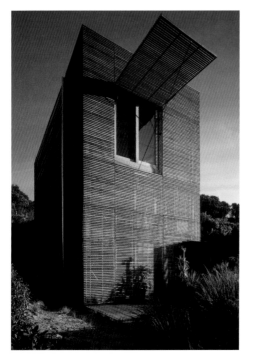

Material impact
Massive in scale and clad entirely in thin strips of timber, the Carter Tucker House, by Australian architect, Sean Godsell, has no outward display of ornamentation. Instead, the impact of this house in Breamlea, Victoria, is through material use and the way in which the sun plays upon and through the slatted timber façade, creating an ethereal beauty.

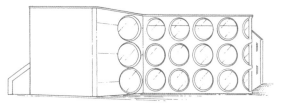

Sculptural façade (left)

Making an artistic statement with the façade of a building is bound to produce a dramatic effect. In Vierwaldstättersee, Switzerland, the aptly named O House, by Philippe Stuebi and Eberhard Tröger, uses a simple circular motif to turn a wall into a vast sculpture.

Decorative screens

Getting creative with concrete was one of the few exceptions to Modernists' distaste for fanciful flourishes. During the 1940s and 50s in particular, architects used decorative concrete block walls, most often with geometric patterns, to create both sun and privacy screens for the exterior of their houses.

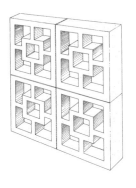

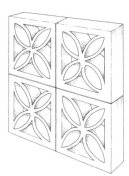

Postmodern irony

Where a Modernist would have used rectangular or ribbon windows, the Postmodern answer is to ham it up with windows in the shape of conventional houses, on a house that itself doesn't feature the pitched roof that every glazed opening has. Even the shelter above the doorway is crooked on this comical Japanese rendition of Postmodernism.

Interior Design

Warm wood

With its many textures and hues wood is a wonderful material to live within. Its colours are predominantly warm and so although wooden floors, furniture and walls are hardwearing they give the impression of comfort. Modernist houses often set wood against colder materials such as steel and concrete.

Interior design in Modernist houses tends to follow one of two trends. It will either be white walled and then scattered with furniture pieces by design icons, often in bright colour; or the interior will be totally designed by the architect and therefore typically minimal in its accoutrements, so as not to distract from the architecture. Either way, order is the word of the day. The idea that the occupant can have many possessions and lots of clutter is either ignored or designed for, with lots of hidden places in which to conceal the detritus of everyday life.

Second-floor plan

Floors: asphalt tile, carpet
Walls: wood
Ceiling: wood

Sleeping porch

Bath

Sleeping porch

Minimal clutter

Typical of the strict early Modernist ideal, the 1922 Schindler House, West Hollywood, by Rudolf Schindler, takes an absolute minimal approach. The main living area, for example, has a bench, a rug and a single small sofa. The fireplace is level with the concrete floor and the walls are unadorned concrete. The effect is austere in the extreme.

Cool concrete

In contrast to wood, concrete is a cold material, both physically and emotionally. While Modernist architects love to use it and to flaunt its use in their finished schemes, it takes a special, architecture-loving person to live day in day out within a house walled in exposed concrete.

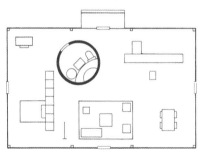

Open-plan layout

Open plan is not a strictly Modernist design ideal but it is one that the genre's architects have taken and run with. Modernist turned Postmodernist Philip Johnson designed his Glass House in New Canaan, Connecticut, with only the bathroom screened by a wall – a circular one. All other rooms were open plan and visible through glazed walls.

Floating staircase

Stripping any element of the house back to its necessary constituent parts is a favourite Modernist approach. The staircase is no exception, with architects designing flights of concrete stairs that have nothing but treads (the part you step on) protruding from a wall. Gone are the vertical risers, the balustrade and outer supporting stair string.

Introduction

Kit houses have been around for a long time. Since the early 20th century companies on both sides of the Atlantic have been designing and selling kits of parts from which an owner or a professional could build a home. This style of buying and building houses became particularly popular in the United States in the 1920s and it still holds a percentage of the new house market today, with major companies offering many sizes and styles of house kit. However, the idea of a kit house has different connotations to different generations. While initially the model evolved to satisfy commercial need and desire for attractive but affordable homes, the Second World War put tremendous strain on governments as bombing created major housing shortages. Kit houses, such as the UK's Airey House, were seen as the answer, providing low cost, quick-build houses for cities and also in poor rural areas. The utilitarian design was an early success and many Airey Houses, built from prefabricated concrete columns and beams onto which shiplap-style concrete panels were fixed, sprang up throughout the UK. However, over time the concrete decayed and a lack of insulation made the houses unattractive to new generations of prospective homeowner.

Postwar prefabs
Designed by Sir Edwin Airey for a Ministry of Works programme, the Airey House was a postwar solution to a cash-strapped British government under pressure to address the need for affordable homes. While most are being either demolished or entirely refurbished, a few have been rescued to serve as a monument to typical postwar urban development.

While homes such as the Airey House have become outdated – with inefficient modes of construction and poor energy efficiency by today's standards – companies still design and build kit houses for markets around the world. In North America dedicated companies sell thousands of house kits each year. In Europe, however, the tendency towards brick-built houses, rather than timber construction, has until recently limited the demand for kit houses... that is until Swedish home products giant IKEA stepped into the market.

The BoKlok concept is a franchise that produces timber-framed terraced houses and apartment buildings for groups of buyers. It is currently being offered in Sweden, Denmark, Norway, Finland, Great Britain and Germany. BoKlok is a relatively new concept and it enters a market that is becoming ever-busier, with different kits and prefabricated houses being offered by large companies and small innovative designers. The houses being produced offer the highest energy efficiency, best factory standard construction and good economic value. Even the staid English attitude of 'brick is best' is being challenged by houses that are designed and built quickly and efficiently to the highest 21st-century standards.

The IKEA effect

Like the Airey House before it, the BoKlok was seen as a quick, low-cost solution to rising demands for housing. Swedish company IKEA recognised a need for such houses and so designed them in their own inimitable Scandinavian style.

Archetypes

Catalogue homes

The Sears Modern Home came in many shapes and sizes, and, if a purchaser wanted to adapt a design, the company would assist and tailor its models accordingly. Parts, including all fixings, were then packaged up and shipped via railway anywhere in the United States, just as other Sears products were delivered to their buyers.

Between 1908, when Sears Roebuck & Company first offered its mail-order home, and 1940, the firm sold over 70,000 houses. There were 447 different designs, from a grand multi-storey house to a small cottage with no bathroom, suitable for summer vacationers. Sears states on its website that it was not an innovative home designer but what it offered was economy of scale. Buyers could afford these kit houses, and, with help from friends, they could build them quickly and cheaply. The mail-order company stayed abreast of new trends and offered customers designs accordingly. It even enabled homeowners to afford central heating, a radical new development in the early 20th century.

Off-the-shelf individuality

Pioneer is a two-bedroom house by Canadian designer Form & Forest. It offers the latest in contemporary design without the high cost of bespoke architecture. The prefabricated house is one of a range of designs available to suit a range of budgets. It is one of a number of architecturally designed prefabricated house options now challenging the traditional kit house market.

Single box solutions

Loft Cube, by Werner Aisslinger, is a super-compact living module that the designer sees as the answer to many commuters' nightmare drive home from the city. The Loft Cube is a one-bedroom apartment, packaged in its own funky shell, which can be sited on existing buildings or within a tiny city lot.

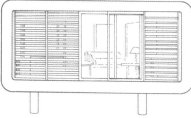

Rustic kits

Not everyone wants an ultra-modern kit house and Live Edge from California offers a more traditional ideal, based upon a classic post-and-beam design. The compact design includes two storeys and multiple rooms, all bundled within a timber-framed and clad façade.

Archetypes

Tradition in a box
The Guildcrest Home comes in many styles but all are based upon traditional designs that the company knows appeal to a majority of buyers. While the rural models such as this example, with their large, glazed gable to the fore, are easy to spot, some of the other less grand models look like any common contractor-built house.

While Sears stopped selling kit houses many years ago, new companies sprang up to take its place in the US and Canadian markets. Their houses are often easily identifiable due to their multi-pitched roofs and abundance of white-framed windows. Viceroy and Guildcrest are two leading modular house manufacturers in Canada, where there is a strong market for this type of house. Both offer modular kits to be built onto foundations already laid by the property owner and local contractors. While the phrase 'kit house' sounds like a temporary measure, these houses are designed to last a lifetime and buyers often select them because they know the material and build quality of the house will be to a recognised standard.

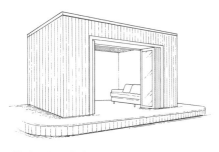

Modernist solutions

The Qube, a British design, is not a house on its own but a modern way of adding space to your home by means of today's growing modular building market. The Qube is a cube, of any size, according to the customer's requirements, that can be adjoined to an existing property or simply set in isolation to create a new office, bedroom, or play space.

Round results

While most houses are versions of a cube, precision engineering now allows companies such as Deltec Homes of Asheville, North Carolina, to offer something different. The panelised building system that the kit arrives as is easy to erect and the circular shape makes such houses more resistant to both hurricanes and earthquakes.

Japanese innovation

As Japan is a small island nation with a large population, its designers are always innovating with new small kit houses. The Dome House is built not of wood, metal or concrete but expanded polystyrene, making it very lightweight and easily assembled. Its shape protects against earthquakes and the internal form promotes air circulation, reducing the need for air conditioning.

Pop-up prefab

House Port is a New York company offering unusual prefabricated designs that are intended for warm, relatively dry climates. The kits consist of living cubes, built from structurally insulated panels, cloaked in a 'port'. The area between the two elements allows air to flow through, cooling the local environment, while the simplicity of construction makes for a fast build.

Lustron House (1950)

Metal dreams

The Lustron House at 411 Bowser Avenue, Chesterton, in Porter County, Indiana, is a surviving example of this 1940s government-backed modular initiative. Its simple rectangular form, designed by Carl Strandlund, makes it inexpensive to erect onto a simple concrete pad foundation.

While in the UK the Airey House was seen as the solution to a housing crisis following the Second World War, in America Lustron Houses were developed to serve the same need. Radically different from conventional houses, their steel frames and baked-porcelain-finished metal panel walls were touted as maintenance-free. The Lustron Corporation forecast that it would build over 40,000 houses in its first two years of production. In reality, only 3,000 were built. However, Lustron has its fans and examples of the houses can still be found today, upholding the company's original mantra of houses that would defy 'weather, wear and time'.

Ranch recall

With a simple gable end and low-pitched roof the Lustron House takes its design aesthetic from the predominant US Ranch style. The differences are obvious though, the metal wall panels and steel-framed windows setting this house apart from its conventional neighbours.

Interior

Designed for the modern family, the Lustron house had low-maintenance walls and ceilings constructed of metal panels. The living arrangement was open plan in part and doors slid into wall pockets rather than swinging open, and creating dead space within the compact house design.

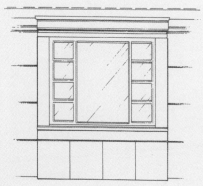

Windows

The large window units consisted of a central fixed pane flanked by two opening lights, each with four smaller panes of glass. The frame is pressed steel and the entire unit sits within a specially designed window module, manufactured to slot neatly into the patented metal wall panels.

Materials & Construction

Engineered style
The Huf Haus is a timber-framed modular house developed by the German company of the same name. Its style is distinct from any other manufacturer and the engineered timber is a focal point of the design. The Huf Haus is the Modernists' ideal made into kit form.

There is no predominant material or construction technique associated with kit houses, as manufacturers and designers have always innovated and are still constantly doing so. This is the essence of the evolution of kit houses – the advancement of technologies and the application of processes to help build better, quicker, more efficient houses to live in. Common to all kit houses is the accuracy with which they are made. Almost all are built from factory-made parts, enabling the manufacturers to work to much smaller tolerances than the trades-people on a construction site. Take the German Huf Haus, for example; an entire house is built from scratch in a week, to the highest possible standards.

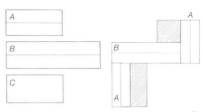

Living containers

Kit houses can come as a trailer load of pieces of timber and a box of fixing devices. They can also come virtually complete, as did this example from Brittany constructed out of two shipping containers. Crossbox House, by French architects Clément Gillet, was built and finished off-site and delivered and lifted into position on-site, the only requirements being connection to local water and electricity supplies.

Adaptable designs

Modular houses are often advertised by their makers as a range of different models. However, the word 'modular' means that with little difficulty the designs should be adaptable to suit the individual's needs. Sears was able to offer this service in the 1920s and good modular house designers can also do so today.

Delivered complete

Like the Crossbox, the Espace Mobile from Austria comes complete to site. This prefabricated house is entirely finished remotely and then delivered to site on a truck. With the foundations complete, it can be lifted into position, connected to services and made habitable in 48 hours.

Eco-friendly solutions

Soe Ker Tie Hias (Butterfly House), by the Norwegian practice TYIN Tegnestue Architects, is a solution to the needs of impoverished Thai people. The wood, metal and bamboo prefabs are a radical example of how kit houses can be designed to suit almost any type of situation.

Doors & Windows

Traditional-style doorway

No one would know that this is a prefab house, nor that its architectural elements, such as the door and porch, were not built in the same way as those on a traditional site-erected house. The difference is that the door was probably installed in the wall before the house was even built.

Just because a home is a kit house does not mean it has to look different from a traditionally built house. The style of the house and elements such as doors and windows is purely dependent upon the design that the manufacturer is aiming to achieve. The way parts like doors and windows are constructed is often different from traditional methods, as they are built into structural elements such as wall panels before being delivered to site. This means that all weatherproofing is installed to the highest degree of accuracy, making kit houses even better than traditional ones at keeping out the weather.

Sears sash

Looking exactly like a conventional sash window, the Sears sash window was purposely designed to resemble traditional windows of the time. Sears was not in the market for designing innovations. It wanted to provide low-cost houses for the masses and so convention ruled.

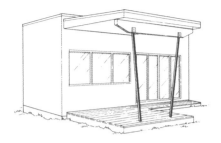

Modern concept entrance

As architectural styles changed, so did the design of kit houses. Today, a modular house is likely to be Modernist in form and feature a flat-roofed porch and glazed door, just as a bespoke architect-designed Modernist house would.

Quirky window designs

The pentagonal windows that are a trademark of Danish company Easy Domes are not a design flourish. They are a product of the geometric nature of the dome-like design of the houses. Hexagonal and pentagonal panels are joined to build the dome houses and some of these panels are glazed.

A wall of windows

When the view is good, then why not glaze the entire wall? While not necessarily energy-efficient, the design of this Jens Risom Prefab House on Block Island, New York State, features an end wall that is split into panels by large structural timbers; the space between each is clad in glass rather than the insulated timber panelling.

Ornamentation

Historic tradition

Aladdin Homes of Michigan, a competitor of Sears Modern Homes, offered a range of traditional kit house styles. Models such as this house, built for Lule Sovereign, secretary-manager of the Aladdin Company, in 1912, harked back to the Arts and Crafts style. The name of this Aladdin model was Brentwood.

The level of ornamentation and decoration that adorns a kit house depends entirely upon the style of home that the manufacturer or designer is aiming to emulate. Houses such as the Sears Modern Home took their reference from existing house styles such as Tudor, Colonial, Federal, Georgian and Victorian. However, the Lustron and Airey houses looked to new materials and technologies for their build and so their appearance was completely different from what people had seen before. Today, kit houses are split between the traditional and modern: both have unique identities and ornamental quirks representative of their styles.

Traditional American siding

Taking the shiplap board as its model, many US kit houses feature 'maintenance-free' plastic siding panels that look as though they are fixed as individual horizontal boards. The effect is traditional, the energy and maintenance factors are modern, and the homeowner gets the best of both worlds.

Log home aesthetic

The log home is perhaps the most romantic of kit houses for those wishing to live in rural North America. Its style and aesthetic hark back to the days of the first European settlers on the continent and the appeal of being surrounded by massive timbers is undeniably comforting. Modern kits have taken this romance and turned it into a viable 21st century home.

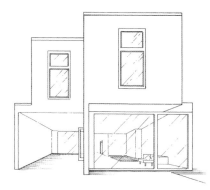

Modern finishes

The variety of external façade finishes for a Modernist kit house is bewildering. From plastics and metal to timber, glass and concrete, there are many materials and effects that can be called upon by today's designers. The overriding factor that binds these varied designs together is the sleekness of finish and concern with clean, uncluttered lines. This is Modernism in kit form.

Interior Design

Simple Modern

Refining the interior design of a kit house to its absolute minimum not only produces a specific aesthetic, it can also reduce costs dramatically. This example uses pale wood tones and white as the predominant decorative finish throughout. The effect is rustic in a very modern way.

The style of a kit house depends entirely upon the decision of the designer or manufacturer. If such a house is to appeal to the mass market then it must be readily acceptable to the majority of people and this means giving them something that they know. With regard to interior design, tradition means moulded trim (skirting and architraves), wooden doors and window frames, stairs with turned balustrades and perhaps even decorative coving to the ceiling edges. However, for every normal kit house there is another of quirky style, and the results are fascinating.

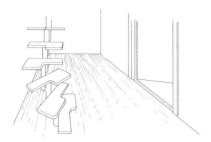

Space-saving

Space saving is often a factor in kit houses, as they are designed to be as economical as possible. Hidden storage spaces are common and quirks such as this minimalistic staircase offer good spatial economy while also looking great. Budding builders should always check safety regulations before building stairways like this though.

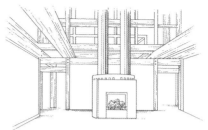

A style of its own

Huf Haus, the German kit house, has a very singular internal aesthetic. Using the timber beams and columns as a framework both structurally and decoratively, the designer has contrasted their dark appearance with white wall panels to create a black and white backdrop on which owners can add their own unique touches.

Swedish style

The interior of an IKEA prefabricated house is very, well, 'IKEA'. Compact in design, the houses are decorated internally by their occupants. However, the defining aesthetic is blond wood and light-coloured wall surfaces that make the rooms feel larger than a dark colour scheme would.

Log cabin tradition

The interior of a log cabin should look pretty similar to the exterior, the walls of massive round logs being the defining aspect of the whole room. This is traditional interior design, colonial settler style, a natural aesthetic that champions the beauty of the trees that were felled to build the house.

Introduction

Unlike the majority of other chapters in this book, there is no one style or defining mantra encompassing 'unusual approaches'. As the title of this chapter suggests, the houses within it are unusual, uncommon, not often seen and definitely not your everyday dwellings. In fact, to hazard a guess, there is perhaps one truly unusually designed and built house for every 100,000 normal houses (the ones that you, I and most of the rest of the world live in).

However, a book about houses would not be complete without a quick look at some of the weirdest and most wonderful; the crazy and the climate-conscious; the quirky and the serious architectural statements. Take, for example, the Steel House, designed and built by artist Robert Bruno. Over twenty years the artist has hoisted and welded chunks of metal, creating this alien-like monument on the edge of Ransom Canyon in Texas. While the Steel House is an artistic statement, many designers use house design to make an architectural statement and to set in stone (or wood or any other material), their beliefs about the profession and how we should aspire to live. These aspirations can be aesthetic (an idealistic vision of the home and life within)

Steel on stilts
Robert Bruno's stegosaurus-like Steel House was conceived not out of the need for a place to live but as an artistic project, one of truly gargantuan proportions that has occupied half a lifetime in its undertaking. Now that's unusual.

Going underground
Using technology first developed to excavate tunnels, Swiss architect Peter Vetsch has created a number of Earth Houses which are, in effect, luxury homes underground. A series of integral arches are formed in sprayed concrete and insulating solid foam is applied to the exterior. The structure is buried in a thick layer of earth, which is subsequently landscaped and grassed over to harmonise with the natural environment.

or functional (a better, more efficient way of conducting our lives, assisted by the house in which we reside). They can, and often do, include ideas on how we can lessen our impact upon the environment through intelligent house design.

This Earth House in Dietikon, Switzerland, one of several designed by architect Peter Vetsch, meets this challenge. While it is undoubtedly unusual and quite charming in appearance, the main design thrust of the house is that it is built into the ground. This endows the house with great thermal stability – the ground insulates the interior against changes in the external temperature and the living quarters remain at a constant, comfortable temperature throughout the year. Additionally, as most of the external structure is also within the earth, it needs no maintenance, apart from the odd run over with the lawnmower! The house is super efficient, requires little energy to heat, and it makes for a great talking point with guests!

Archetypes

Sliding skin

The Sliding House in Suffolk, has a moving façade, a solid external cover that, with the aid of a motorised mechanism, is manoeuvred back and forth over the house. The sliding façade can cover the glazed portion of the house or expose it to the sky, creating a glass living space and open-air bathroom.

What is the archetype for a house designed with an unusual approach? There is none but the following houses are great examples of innovative and quirky design, elements of which can be and often are used on more normal houses that you and I live in. For instance, many houses feature a conservatory or sun room clad in glass but all suffer from that room being cold in winter and too hot in summer. What if you could moderate the amount of glazed façade open to the elements by rolling back the solid walls to uncover the glass? Check out the Sliding House by DRMM.

Floating house

When the land is difficult to build on, where else can a house be put? How about on the water? Floating Home by MOS Architects is a conventionally designed timber house. However, it is built on a floating raft that sits between two islets in Lake Huron, Canada.

Micro living

Reducing the space in which we live is becoming ever more important in the crowded cities of the world. The micro compact home (M-ch), designed by Tech University Munich, takes this idea to the max (or minimum) to create a tiny living space that features all the elements of a conventional-sized house.

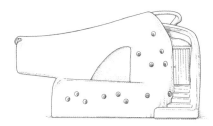

Organic form

Truss Wall House in Tokyo, by Ushida Findlay, is a wonderful example of artistry in architecture and the quest to emulate the beauty of nature in built form. Unlike any other house, this one is an amalgamation of curves and clever ideas that together create a beautiful and unique dwelling, cast in concrete.

Infill architecture

Look closer at any crowded city and there are countless potential plots for houses if you're prepared to think differently. Galley House, by architect Donald Chong, is a super-slim but wonderfully stylish home squeezed between two existing Victorian houses in Toronto. Infill architecture, as it is known, is becoming more common as cities fill up and conventional building plots become rare or too expensive.

Archetypes

Minimalism is an offshoot of the Modernist ideal and one that strips down the architectural requirements for living to the bare minimum. It is not to most people's taste, primarily because living in a Minimalist house requires a lot of discipline. However, architectural purists salivate at houses designed in this way and one of the most admired practising Minimalist architects is Tadao Ando. Renowned for his pared-back designs, Ando works in concrete, creating buildings that defy convention and address anew how we perceive the home, the church, even the busy urban thoroughfare.

Minimal design
Row House, in Osaka, by Tadao Ando, is a minimalist take on a traditional Asian-style house. The narrow front façade gives way to a long, thin building with rooms set in a row going far back into the lot. The blank façade Ando presents is an introduction to a home filled with empty space and tranquility.

Underground living

Villa Ottolenghi in Italy's Veneto region was designed by Carlo Scarpa and completed in 1978. Built into the ground to overcome planning restrictions regarding the height of buildings on the site, the house has only one visible façade.

Fascinating façade

When architects are given free rein, they come up with some wild ideas. In Tokyo the Curtain Wall House, by Shigeru Ban, is a concrete structure with a fabric façade, or curtains for walls. While not viable in most locations, it does illustrate the potential of alternative materials in construction.

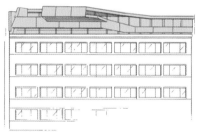

Rock houses

Houses set within rock, some people would call them caves. However, our ancestors were more enterprising than simply moving into a hole in the rock. They carved out rooms and built front façades onto the rock face. They created houses from the very strata that we live upon and evidence for this can be seen at the Rock Houses of Kinver Edge in Worcestershire.

Rooftop living

If cities are filling up where can we build? The answer, according to Austrian architect DMAA, is on top of the existing buildings. Ray 1 is a futuristic apartment home designed and built on top of an ordinary office block in the centre of Vienna.

Fuller Dome Home (1960)

Home from dome
The spherical Fuller Dome Home departed radically from the conventional US house. It used a framework of triangles braced against each other to create a super-strong structure requiring no internal supports. The difficulty came in teaching contractors to build the homes and waterproofing the seams and joints.

The geodesic dome was popularised by R. Buckminster Fuller and he used it throughout his architectural career to create unique buildings. Perhaps the most interesting and enduring of these was the house that he and Anne Hewlett occupied. Located in Carbondale, Illinois, the Fuller Dome Home has been renovated by volunteers to allow visitors to see the unusual house and experience the feeling of living within a property constructed of a complex framework and triangular panels. Fuller designed the home as a quick-build solution to postwar housing shortages, imagining it being flown into hard-to-reach areas in kit form.

External view

The triangulated structure of the Dome Home can be appreciated best from the exterior. While the overall shape is curved, the individual elements are all straight-edged triangles, locked together within the complex framework of rods and nodes (jointing elements).

Internal plan, main floor

The architect designed the interior to be predominantly open plan. The kitchen area abuts a mechanical room, from where all necessary heating and cooking equipment is operated, and the only other closed spaces are the two bathrooms, one each for homeowners and guests.

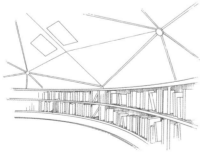

Curved bookshelves

Fitting furniture into a house with no straight walls could be a challenge but Fuller designed to suit his unique house and the upper storey of the interior features a built-in bookcase that hugs the external walls.

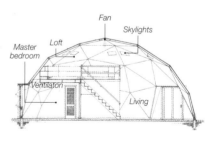

Section view

Taking a slice through the structure of Bucky Fuller's Dome Home illustrates that there are no internal supports. The triangular structure pushes against itself to become self-supporting. This means that any kind of internal layout is possible.

Materials & Construction

Mother Earthship
This earthship is an example of a growing trend in the USA and Europe for houses that demonstrate how we can build sustainably using entirely reclaimed materials. The walls are constructed from recycled tyres filled with a ballast of sand or stones, and glass bottles laid like bricks in lime mortar.

The materials used to make houses become ever more numerous and varied as techniques and technology advance. Where once the idea of building with paper or rubber would have seemed absurd, such materials are now viable options, depending on location and the nature of the construction. As environmental issues grow, natural materials are back in favour. Straw is now more commonly used, as are recycled tyres and plastic and glass bottles, to build strong, durable walls at relatively low cost, which can compete with conventional and even high-tech construction materials in terms of insulation and weatherproofing.

Excavated earth

Built from mud and sticks and stones, this fairytale house is a low-impact environmental house. Constructed by its owner in the UK, the house incorporates the resources from the site around it – tree branches, earth and rocks – plus straw bales and lime plaster. The result is a unique house that meets the highest environmental standards.

Fabric façade

Natural Ellipse, by Japanese architect Masaki Endoh, is a house in Tokyo made of fabric. Unlike the Curtain Wall House (see page 237), it is a fibre-reinforced polymer stretched over laser-cut metal ribs to form a semi-rigid external façade.

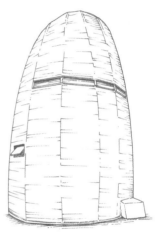

Energy efficient

Environmental design is becoming more common and these houses in Grande Synthe, a suburb of Dunkirk in northern France, are textbook examples. Designed by ZEDfactory, they include super insulation, solar heating and power, natural lighting and ventilation, water recycling and a host of other features that can all be fitted to conventional houses.

Doors & Windows

Doors and windows are important parts of any house, but while a door has one basic use, the window has the potential to fulfil numerous aesthetic and environmental functions. Glazing admits natural light, provides views and can be treated with colours or patterns to create artistic flourishes. The window as a whole can be sealed to maintain constant internal conditions, or may open as an integral part of the breathable environmental envelope of the house. Today glass can even be treated to harness solar power, so becoming a part of the energy strategy of the house.

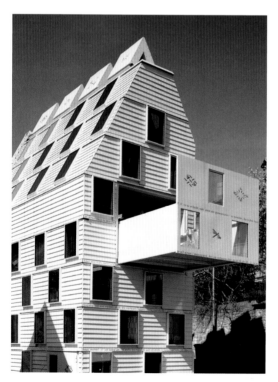

Inside out

Living Room, a house in Gelnhausen, Germany, is designed by Formalhaut, two architects who, with artists and a poet, created this unusual addition to the town's medieval heart. Defying the idea of a house as a private interior, one level slides out like a huge drawer, and a rigorous grid of windows invites any passers-by to peer within.

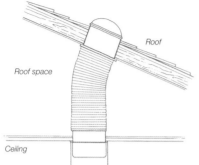

Light from above

Getting natural light deep into the heart of a house, especially one that is built into a hillside or partially underground, is a challenge. The answer is to use a sun tube. This glazed dome sits on the roof, allowing light to shine down a tube lined with a reflective coating, so bouncing natural light right into the darkest corners of the house.

Opening façade

If the view is great, why not open up the entire façade? Chicken Point Cabin, a house by Tom Kundig in Hayden, Idaho, has a glazed wall that pivots open to allow the outside in. The solution is simple and exciting, as all great architectural innovations should be.

Energy-producing window

Advances in photovoltaic technology – the collection of solar energy – mean that houses are now starting to be fitted with solar windows. These glazed elements not only allow light in but they also harness the sun's energy for use as electrical power in the house.

Ornamentation

Building as art

Built not in the 1960s but in 2006, the Nautilus House, by Arquitectura Organica, has no straight walls either inside or out. This house in Mexico City is utterly unique and magical, both for the imagination used to come up with the idea and the skill required to build it.

Ornament is a matter of taste in all things. Ornament on the scale of architecture is a big decision. Perhaps that is why the Modernist movement, with its aversion to overt ornamentation, is so popular. Conversely, many house designers and owners go out of their way to add decoration to their houses and the success of these results varies wildly. Houses deemed as having an unusual approach are bound to produce some extravagant ideas with regards to ornamentation. Take, for example, the Nautilus House in Mexico, modelled on a snail shell, which is more sculpture than architecture.

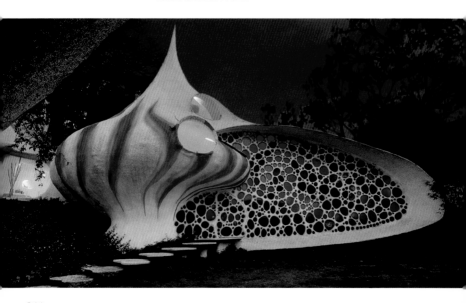

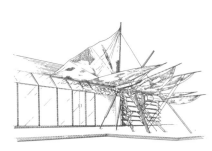

Contemporary canopy

Perhaps this English home is Postmodernist or simply very different. The Butterfly House in Godalming, Surrey, designed by Laurie Chetwood, is inspired by the lifecycle of the butterfly, but it uses high-tech and industrial materials to achieve the design.

Cast concrete

A Modernist house is made different by the inclusion of an unusually shaped façade on its upper storey. Instead of a blank concrete wall, the architect has formed a triangulated ripple effect, which enlivens the façade and intrigues passers-by.

Chimney sculpture

No architect is more famous for sculptural design than Antoni Gaudí. The Spanish master of the wow factor included sculpture in all parts of his designs, including rooftop chimney pots such as these on Casa Milà, an apartment block in central Barcelona.

Living walls

Once it was ivy growing up a cottage wall; now architects are incorporating plants as part of the decorative, and environmental, design for the exterior of buildings. Living walls and green roofs have sustainability credentials and look fabulous too.

Interior Design

Round about

Designed by Antti Lovag, Bubble Palace outside Cannes on the French Riviera is a structure of domes, its interior as curvaceous as the external shell. Resembling something out of a film set, the house is littered with designer furniture and quirky touches such as unusually shaped arches, circular alcoves and curved walls.

As with ornamentation, the interior design of houses created by designers who have taken an unusual approach can include just about anything: there is no set of architectural rules or values to abide by. The results are many and varied – from the utterly outlandish to the unique and innovative. Some are suitable only for the house for which they have been designed, others are clever ideas that can be taken up in more ordinary houses, design quirks that we would all be keen to integrate into our lifestyles. The Bubble Castle in the south of France, built in the 1970s, is one of the former: a remarkable house with an interior so utterly unique that it would fit nowhere else.

Adaptable interior

Transforming from a one-room pavilion with windows on all sides into a compartmentalised house with bedrooms, bathroom and living spaces, Suitcase House, near Beijing, China, by Edge Design, uses folding, lifting and lowering panels to split the overall space and reveal secret rooms otherwise hidden within the internal structure of the house.

Recycled décor

The saying 'one man's trash is another man's treasure' fits this house perfectly. All kinds of scrap has been used to build and decorate the house. Recycled bottles, corks, tile colour samples and more adorn the interior of the house, making unique and beautiful decorative additions.

Wooden wallpaper

Logs, cut through and formed into panels showing the end grain, form a series of panels that together create a stunning wall covering. The idea is not unique but the results are very different and add a rich, warm feel to the interior design.

Stairway shift

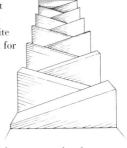

Taking an element and subverting its design is a favourite architectural trick for interiors – curved walls, hidden spaces, etc – but the staircase is most often standard. Not here; this wonderfully playful creation makes for a great interior design piece, although how easy it is to climb is debatable.

Glossary

ACANTHUS a plant with deeply divided leaves whose form is used as an architectural motif.

AMERICAN COLONIAL architectural movement encompassing several styles built by settlers between the 16th and 19th centuries.

ANTIQUITY the ancient Greek and Roman periods.

APEX the pointed top of a gable or pediment.

APPLIED made separately and added later.

ARCADE a row of arches.

ARCH a curved opening.

ARCHITRAVE the lowest component of a Classical entablature; also the frame around an opening.

ARTS AND CRAFTS international design movement championing traditional crafts, c. 1860–1910.

ASHLAR stone masonry of regular blocks.

ASTRAGAL a half-round moulding.

ATRIUM an open-roofed entrance hall or central court.

ATTACHED *see* ENGAGED

BALCONY a projecting gallery or walkway.

BALUSTER a vertical shaft supporting a rail.

BALUSTRADE a row of balusters topped by a rail.

BARGEBOARD a decorative board covering the angled sides of a roof gable.

BAROQUE the extravagant European architectural style of the 17th and 18th centuries.

BASE the lower part of a column.

BAY the vertical division of a building, often by windows or arches.

BEAM a horizontal structural support.

BLIND ARCADE a blank arcade, without openings.

BOND a pattern of laying bricks.

BOW WINDOW a curved bay window.

BRACE a diagonal support linking a series of uprights.

BUTTRESS a mass of masonry built against a wall to reinforce it.

CANOPY a projecting ornamental hood.

CANTED angled.

CANTILEVER an overhanging projection with no support on its outside edge.

CAPITAL the top of a column.

CASEMENT WINDOW a window with hinged panes.

CEMENT a lime-based paste that binds together and sets hard; it is used in mortar, concrete and as render.

CHAMFER a bevelled edge.

CLADDING an exterior covering.

CLAPBOARD a type of wooden siding.

CLASSICAL pertaining to the ancient Greek and Roman periods.

CLERESTORY a row of high-level windows.

CLOSERS short bricks or stones around an opening.

COFFERING a pattern of sunken panels.

COLONETTE a small column.

COLONNADE a row of columns.

COLUMN a freestanding shaft, often supporting an arch or entablature.

CONCRETE a mixture of cement and aggregate (sand and stones) that dries very hard; it is used as a building material.

CORBEL a projecting block or capital supporting an arch or shaft above.

CORINTHIAN one of the five Classical orders.

CORNICE a horizontal projecting moulding, especially the topmost component of an entablature.

CRAFTSMAN *see* ARTS AND CRAFTS

CRENELLATION *see* BATTLEMENT

CRUCIFORM cross-shaped.

CUPOLA a small decorative form of dome.

CURTAIN WALL a thin, non-structural wall in front of a structural frame.

DORIC one of the five Classical orders.

DORMER a window projecting from a roof.

DOUBLE-HUNG WINDOW a sash window with two sliding sections.

DRY STONE WALLING masonry made without mortar.

EAVES the part of a roof that projects beyond the wall.

EGG-AND-DART a type of moulding resembling egg shapes alternating with dart shapes.

ELEVATION any of the vertical faces of a building, inside or out.

ENGAGED (of a column) attached to the wall.

ENTABLATURE the whole of the horizontal structure above the capitals in a Classical order.

FAÇADE an exterior face of a building.

FANLIGHT a semicircular window over a door.

FEDERAL STYLE American neoclassical architecture of *c*. 1776–*c*.1830.

FIELDED PANEL a square or rectangular panel with a raised central section.

FINIAL the decorative knob on top of a gable, post or other upright.

FLUE the pipe inside a chimney to conduct smoke outwards.

FLUTING parallel concave channels on a column or surface.

FRAMING a structural skeleton in wood or metal.

FRIEZE a decorative horizontal band, especially the central component of an entablature.

FRENCH DOORS OR WINDOWS full-length casement windows opening like doors onto a balcony or terrace.

FRESCO a painting made with pigment applied directly into wet plaster.

GABLE the flat pointed end wall of a pitched roof.

GALLERY an internal passage, usually open on one side.

GEORGIAN English architectural style of *c*. 1700–1840.

GIANT ORDER an arch encompassing two or more storeys.

GLAZED made of glass; glossy.

GLAZING BAR *see* MUNTIN

GOTHIC European architectural style of *c*. 1150–*c*.1500.

GOTHIC REVIVAL a late 18th- and 19th-century Gothic-inspired style.

GREEK the style current in ancient Greece from the 7th to 2nd centuries BC.

GREEK REVIVAL a late 18th- and early 19th-century style drawing on ancient Greek examples.

HALF-TIMBERED having exposed timber framing.

HALL an entranceway; also the main room of a medieval house.

HAMMERBEAM a short roof timber cantilevered out to carry an upright.

HEARTH a fireproof floor area for making a fire.

HIPPED ROOF a roof that is pitched at the ends as well as the sides.

HOOD MOULDING a three-sided moulding over a window or door; also called drip moulding.

INFILL material used to fill spaces between the components of a framework.

IONIC one of the five Classical orders.

JAMB the vertical part of a door or window opening.

JETTY an overhanging upper storey.

JOIST a horizontal timber supporting a floor or ceiling.

KEYSTONE the central block locking together an arch.

LANCET a tall, narrow, pointed, early Gothic window.

LANTERN a turret or tower on top of a roof or dome to let in light.

LIGHT the vertical section of a window.

LINTEL the beam over an opening, supported on jambs or columns.

LOUVRE a small structure or opening for ventilation.

LUNETTE a half-round window.

MANTEL a lintel or shelf above a fireplace.

MANTELPIECE the decorative structure around a fireplace.

MASON someone who builds in stone or brick.

MASONRY stone or brick construction.

MEANDER a snaking pattern of straight lines joined at angles.

MEDIEVAL the period in European history spanning *c*. 1000–*c*. 1500.

Glossary

MODERNIST the architectural style current from *c.* 1920 to the late 20th century.

MOULDING a strip with a shaped or decorated surface.

MORTAR a paste made of lime or cement, used in between blocks or bricks.

MORTISE a hole or slot for a tenon, which is used to join wood pieces.

MOSAIC a picture made of tiny coloured tiles.

MOTIF a decorative element, usually repeated.

MULLION a vertical element dividing a window into sections.

MUNTIN a small vertical or horizontal wooden bar holding the panes in a sash window; also called a glazing bar.

NATURALISTIC lifelike.

NEOCLASSICAL an architectural style based on Classical precedents, which was fashionable in the 18th and early 19th centuries.

NEWEL the central post of a spiral stair, or the endpost of a straight stair.

NICHE an ornamental recess, often curved at the back and top.

OCULUS a round window.

OGEE a shallow reverse-curve or S-curve.

ORDERS the five accepted styles of Classical columns and entablatures.

ORIEL a bay window starting above ground level.

PALLADIAN in the style of Italian architect Andrea Palladio (1508–1580).

PALLADIAN WINDOW an opening with two straight sidelights whose entablatures support a central arched opening.

PANELLING a decorative wooden or plaster wall covering with areas defined by mouldings.

PARAPET the edge of a wall, projecting above roof level.

PEDESTAL the substructure below a column or supporting a statue.

PEDIMENT the gable above a Classical portico; also a gable form used decoratively.

PERPENDICULAR a 15th-century style of English Gothic architecture, characterised by panelled effects on walls and windows.

PILASTER a flat column form, usually attached to a wall.

PILLAR a column or pier.

PINNACLE an ornamental structure, usually pointed, on top of a buttress or other structure.

PITCH the slope of a roof.

PLAN a drawing or horizontal section showing the arrangement of spaces in a building.

PLASTER finely ground lime or gypsum paste used for interior wall finishings.

PLATE GLASS large sheet glass.

PLINTH a plain projecting support at the bottom of a wall, column or other upright.

PORCH a partially enclosed space in front of a door.

PORTAL a door.

PORTE-COCHÈRE a covered passage allowing access for vehicles, or an open porch large enough to drive under.

PORTICO a covered area with a colonnaded front.

POST a vertical timber support.

PRAIRIE STYLE an American architectural style of the late 19th and early 20th centuries.

PURLIN a horizontal beam along the length of a roof.

QUEEN ANNE an eclectic 19th-century style with mixed Gothic and Baroque detailing.

QUOIN large block used to strengthen angles and corners.

RAFTER a long, angled roof timber supporting the covering.

RENAISSANCE the revival of Classical forms and learning in Italy in the 15th and 16th centuries, and in the 16th and 17th centuries in northern Europe.

RENDER a paste of cement and aggregate (sand or stones) used as a waterproof wall covering; also called stucco.

REVEAL the vertical inner face of an opening.

RIB an arched moulding on a vault.

RIDGE the top edge of a roof.

RISER the vertical part of a step.

ROCOCO a light and delicate 18th-century style.

ROMAN pertaining to ancient Rome, and especially the Roman Empire, 27 BC–330 AD.

ROMANESQUE the architectural style of *c.* 1000–1200 AD; also known as Norman in England and Normandy.

ROTUNDA a circular room.

ROUNDEL a small circular frame or motif.

RUBBLE masonry with irregularly shaped blocks.

RUSTICATION masonry cut so that the centre of each block projects.

SASH WINDOW a window with vertically (or occasionally horizontally) sliding wooden frames holding the glass panes.

SCAGLIOLA a paste made of pigment, plaster and glue.

SCROLL an S-shaped curve.

SHAFT the cylindrical body of a column.

SHINGLE a wooden tile; also a late 19th-century American architectural variation of the Queen Anne style.

SHUTTERS wooden doors used to cover a window.

SIDING an exterior wall covering made of parallel strips of wood or other materials.

SOFFIT the underside of an architectural structure, such as an arch.

SPANDREL the triangular area between an arch and its rectangular surround.

SPLAY an angled surface.

STAINED GLASS coloured glass.

STANCHION An upright bar, beam, post, or support.

STOREY a level, or floor, of a building.

STRAPWORK a decorative pattern resembling leather straps.

STRING the diagonal side of a staircase; it can be closed (solid) or open (showing the ends of the treads and risers).

STRING COURSE a raised horizontal moulding that visually divides storeys; also called a plat band.

STRUCTURAL FRAME The construction elements that combine to provide support for the entire building.

STUCCO *see* **RENDER**

STYLISED abstract or symbolic in depiction.

SURROUND a frame or an architrave.

TENON the projection inserted into a mortise to join two pieces of wood.

TERRACOTTA A hard, fired clay brownish-red in colour when unglazed. It is used for architectural ornaments and facings, structural units, pottery, and as a material for sculpture.

TERRACE a row of houses joined together; a raised platform in a garden.

TORUS a half-round or roll moulding.

TRACERY the decorative stone bars in a Gothic window.

TRANSOM horizontal bar across a window; also the upper part of a door frame.

TREAD the horizontal part of a step.

TUDOR the period of English history from 1485 to 1603.

TURRET a small tower, especially one starting above ground level.

TUSCAN one of the five Classical orders.

VALANCE the fabric or wooden covering above a window; also called a pelmet.

VAULT a curved stone ceiling.

VICTORIAN pertaining to the reign of Queen Victoria, 1837–1901.

VILLA a country house or suburban house.

WEATHERBOARDING a type of wooden siding.

WING the side part of a building.

Directory of Houses

This listing includes featured houses in the UK and Europe that are open to the public, together with a selection from North America and Australia.

HOUSES TO VISIT IN THE UK

ASCOTT HOUSE
Leighton Buzzard, Bedfordshire
www.ascottestate.co.uk

BISHOP'S HOUSE
Sheffield, South Yorkshire
www.museums-sheffield.org.uk

DIMBOLA LODGE
Freshwater, Isle of Wight
www.dimbola.co.uk

GEORGIAN HOUSE MUSEUM
Great George Street, Bristol
www.bristol.gov.uk

HAMPTON COURT PALACE
Hampton Court, Surrey
www.hrp.org.uk

HARDWICK HALL
Doe Lea, Chesterfield
www.nationaltrust.org.uk

HILL HOUSE
Helensburgh, Glasgow, Scotland
www.nts.org.uk

KEATS HOUSE
Hampstead, London
www.stately-homes.com

KEDLESTON HALL
Derby, Derbyshire
www.nationaltrust.org.uk

KELMSCOTT MANOR
Kelmscott, Lechdale, Oxfordshire
www.kelmscottmanor.co.uk

KINVER EDGE AND ROCK HOUSES
Kinver, Stourbridge, Worcestershire
www.nationaltrust.org.uk

LITTLE MORETON HALL
Moreton, Cheshire
www.nationaltrust.org.uk

MAX GATE
Higher Bockhampton, Dorset
www.nationaltrust.org.uk

PENDEAN FARMHOUSE
Singleton, West Sussex
www.wealddown.co.uk

PORT SUNLIGHT
Wirral, Merseyside
www.portsunlightvillage.com

QUEEN ELIZABETH'S HUNTING LODGE
Chingford, Essex
www.cityoflondon.gov.uk

THE QUEEN'S HOUSE
Greenwich, London
www.rmg.co.uk

RED HOUSE
Bexleyheath, Kent
www.nationaltrust.org.uk

SALTRAM HOUSE
Merafield Road, Plymouth
www.nationaltrust.org.uk

ST FAGANS (NATIONAL MUSEUM WALES)
Cardiff, Wales
www.museumwales.ac.uk

SUTTON HOUSE
Hackney, London
www.nationaltrust.org.uk

HOUSES TO VISIT IN EUROPE
Czech Republic

MUZEUM JUDR. OTAKARA KUDRNY
Netolice
muzeum.netolice.cz

France

MAISON MANTIN
Place du Colonel Laussedat Moulins
www.moulins-tourisme.com

PETIT TRIANON
Versailles
en.chateauversailles.fr

PLACE DES VOSGES
75004 Paris
(Public space; Victor Hugo's house/
museum at No. 6)

ST SULPICE DE GRIMBOUVILLE
Eure
www.normandie-tourisme.fr/
Maison-medievale-de-St-Sulpice-de-
Grimbouville

VILLA SAVOYE
Rue de Villiers, Poissy
www.villa-savoye.monuments-
nationaux.fr

Germany

THE MASTERS' HOUSES
Ebertallee, Dessau
www.meisterhaeuser.de

Italy

MEDICI VILLA DI POGGIO
Poggio a Caiano, Prato
www.museumsinflorence.com

PALAZZO FARNESE
00100 Rome
www.inventerome.com

PALAZZO GADDI
Florence, Tuscany
www.capodannoinfirenze.com

PALLADIO CORNARO VILLA
Piombino Dese, Padua
musei.provincia.padova.it

VILLA CAPRA LA ROTONDA
Vicenza, Veneto
www.villalarotonda.it

Villa Medici di Fiesole
Fiesole, Florence, Tuscany
www.cultura.toscana.it

The Netherlands

BARTOLOTTI HOUSE
Sarphatistraat, Amsterdam
www.theaterinstituut.nl

EDAM MUSEUM
Edam, Damplein
www.edamsmuseum.nl

Spain

CASA MILÀ (LA PEDRERA)
Provença, Barcelona
www.barcelona.com
ANTONI GAUDÍ

CASITA DEL PRINCIPE
El Pardo, Madrid
www.spain.info

CASA VICENS
Carrer de les Carolines 24, Barcelona
(Exterior only)

HOUSES TO VISIT IN AUSTRALIA

ELIZABETH BAY HOUSE
Elizabeth Bay, New South Wales
www.hht.net.au

ROSE SEIDLER HOUSE
Wahroonga, Sydney
www.hht.net.au

HOUSES TO VISIT IN NORTH AMERICA

Canada

THE GRANGE
(ART GALLERY OF ONTARIO)
Toronto, Ontario
www.ago.net

USA

BUCKMINSTER FULLER DOME HOME
Carbondale, IL
www.fullerdomehome.org

CONFERENCE HOUSE
Tottenville, Staten Island, NY
www.conferencehouse.org

EAMES HOUSE
Pacific Palisades, Los Angeles, CA
eamesfoundation.org

FALLINGWATER
Bear Run, Pittsburgh, PA
www.fallingwater.org

FARNSWORTH HOUSE
River Road, Plano, IL
www.farnsworthhouse.org

FRANK LLOYD WRIGHT HOME & STUDIO
Chicago Ave, Oak Park, IL
gowright.org

GAMBLE HOUSE
Westmoreland Place, Pasadena, CA
www.gamblehouse.org

GLASS HOUSE
Elm Street, New Canaan, CT
philipjohnsonglasshouse.org

GRACELAND
Elvis Presley Blvd, Memphis, TN
www.elvis.com/graceland

MARK TWAIN HOUSE
Farmington Ave, Hartford, CT
www.marktwainhouse.org

MONTICELLO
Charlottesville, VA
www.monticello.org

NEUTRA HOUSE
Silver Lake Blvd, Los Altos, CA
www.neutrahouse.org

F. C. ROBIE HOUSE
Woodlawn Ave, Chicago, IL
gowright.org

ROSE HILL MANOR
Rose Hill Manor Pk, Frederick, MD
www.rosehillmuseum.com

STAHL HOUSE
Woods Drive, Los Angeles, CA
www.stahlhouse.com

CURRENT ARCHITECTS & PRACTICES FEATURED

24H ARCHITECTURE
www.24h.eu

AIRES MATEUS & ASSOCIATES
www.airesmateus.com

WERNER AISSLINGER
www.aisslinger.de

TADAO ANDO
www.andotadao.org

ARQUITECTURA ORGANICA
www.arquitecturaorganica.com

BRUNO BLESCH
www.ueber-bau.de

ALBERTO CAMPO BAEZA
www.campobaeza.com

CG ARCHITECTES
www.cgarchitectes.fr

LAURIE CHETWOOD
www.chetwoods.com

DONALD CHONG
www.williamsonchong.com

COOPER JOHNSON SMITH
www.cjsarch.com

DMAA
www.deluganmeissl.at

DRMM
www.drmm.co.uk

DVA ARHITEKTA
www.dva-arhitekta.hr

EDGE DESIGN
www.commune.com.cn

USHIDA FINDLAY
www.ushida-findlay.com

FORM & FOREST
www.formandforest.com

FORMALHAUT
www.formalhaut.de

FRANK GEHRY
www.foga.com/

FAT
www.fashionarchitecturetaste.com

SEAN GODSELL ARCHITECTS
www.seangodsell.com

BERNALTE LEÓN Y ASOCIADOS
www.bernalteleon.com

JERGEN H. MAYER
www.jmayerh.de

MOUNT FUJI ARCHITECTS
www.14.plala.or.jp/mfas/fuji.htm

JM ARCHITECTURE
www.jma.it

JUAN CARLOS DOBLADO
www.juancarlosdoblado.com

TOM KUNDIG
www.olsonkundigarchitects.com

OMA/REM KOOLHAAS
www.oma.eu

LIVE EDGE
www.liveedge-prefab.com

MOS ARCHITECTS
www.mos-office.ne

QUBE
www.theqube.co.uk

GUILDCREST HOMES
www.www.guildcrest.com

DELTEC HOMES
www.deltechomes.com

JAPAN DOME HOUSE
www.i-domehouse.com

HOUSE PORT
www.ehouseport.com

JENS RISOM
www.jensrisom.com.com

SANTAMBROGIO MILANO
www.santambrogiomilano.it

SHIGERU BAN
www.shigerubanarchitects.com

KEN SHUTTLEWORTH
www.makearchitects.com

SOU FUJIMOTO ARCHITECTS
www.sou-fujimoto.net

**PHILIPPE STUEBI &
EBERHARD TRÖGER**
www.philippestuebi.ch

SUPERKÜL
www.superkul.ca

BING THOM ARCHITECTS
www.bingthomarchitects.com

TYIN TEGNESTUE ARCHITECTS
www.tyintegnestue.no

PETER VETSCH/EARTH HOUSE
www.erdhaus.ch

ZEDFACTORY
www.ruralzed.com

Index

Acknowledgements

Author acknowledgements

I wish to thank Jason Hook, Caroline Earle, Michael Whitehead, Stephanie Evans, Janie Pumfrey and the rest of the team at Ivy Press for their sterling work in taking my building picks and subsequent texts and turning them into this wonderful book. I would also like to acknowledge the many authors, architects and website creators for the wealth of information available to me, which helped in my research for this publication. And lastly, but by no means least, thanks to my wife, Stephanie, for her continual support in all of my endeavours.

The publisher would like to thank the following individuals and organisations for their kind permission to reproduce the images in this book. Every effort has been made to acknowledge the pictures, however we apologise if there are any unintentional omissions.

Adam Architecture/www.adamarchitecture/ Photography by John Critchley: 140. **Alamy/Arcaid Images**: 10, 182; Hemis: 246; International Photobank: 162; Nicholas Kane: 38; David Moore/ Happisburgh: 23; The National Trust Photolibrary: 201. **Tom Arban Photography Inc.**/www. tomarban.com/superkül: 48. **Baker Custom Photo**/www.bakercustomphoto. com: 50. **Shihmei Barger**: 172.

Bill Bertram: 92. **BoKlok**: 217. **Julie Brister**: 44. **Manfred Brückels**: 20. **Steve Cadman**: 154. **Earl Carter**: 212. **Daniel Case**: 2, 108. **Corbis/Mark Fiennes/Arcaid**: 168; Ann Johansson: 206; Lee Snider/Photo Images: 116; Alan Weintraub/Arcaid: 18; Adam Woolfitt: 124. **Brett and Sue Coulstock**: 36. **Heather Cowper**: 134. **Dennis Domer**: 185. **Martin Ely**: 176. **Robert English**: 73. **Terence Faircloth, Atelier Teee, Inc**: 34. **Christophe Finot**: 98. **Flickr**/Chicagogeek: 184; Chillihead: 122; Matahina: 210; Sheffield Tiger: 76. **Fotolia**/William McKelvie: 26. **David Franck Photographie**/www. davidfranck.de: 30. **Frank Gallaugher**: 16. Photo by Ethan Garrett (Flickr. com/ethangarrett): 82. **Getty Images**/Brigitte Merle: 74; Guy Vanderelst: 4. **Ben Godfrey**: 32. **Victor Grigas**: 240. **Graham Hazeldon**: 86. **Carol M. Highsmith**: 202. **Tony Hisgett**: 102, 174. **Historic American Buildings Survey, National Park Service**/Thad Heckman: 239. **Historic-Deerfield**: 114. **Huf-Haus**/http://www.huf-haus.com: 224, 230. **David Illif**: 164. **Andrew Jameson**: 80. **Jacopo Mascheroni**/ JM Architecture: 46. **Oxfordian Kissuth**: 70–1. **Gaby Koch**: 110. **Shannon Kyles**/ ontarioarchitecture.com: 146. **Quirin Leppert**/www.formalhaut.de: 242. **Library of Congress**: 7, 22, 24, 64, 66,

118, 131, 135, 135, 135, 150, 167, 194, 198, 200, 222; Joseph Elliott, HABS photographer: 144; Historic American Buildings Survey (Library of Congress): 166. Photography by **Francisco Lubbert**/ Design by Javier Senosiain: 244. **Takato Marui**: 6. **David Marvin**: 226, 228. **Cory Maylett**: 156. **Donata Mazzini**: 90. **Hiromitsu Morimoto**: 236. **Laura Nolte**: 126. **Openroads.com**: 105. **Dave Parker**: 192. **Stephen Parker**: 216. **Hazel Phillips**: 11. **Pro-Fab/Guildcrest Homes**: 220. **Jesse Raeen**: 100. **The RBF Dome NFP**: 238. **Niccolò Rigacci**: 89. **Paul Roberts**: 160. **Hans A. Rosbach**: 137. **Eric Allix Rogers**: 40. **Ross Russell**/ www.therussellhouse.org: 234. **Stefan Scheer**: 178. **Ivo Shandor**: 186. **Shutterstock**/Dhoxax: 60; Federicofoto: 94; Katatonia82: 214; Monbibi: 58; Pack-Shot: 96; Zacarias Pereira da Mata: 62; Polin: 54; Sylvana Rega: 159; Jane Rix: 72; Sergieiev: 68; Tupungato: 42. **Brian Snelson**: 28. **Ilpo's Sojourn**: 208. **Dominic Stone**: 169. **Ken'ichi Suzuki**/Mount Fuji Architects Studio: 204. **William Warby**: 78. **Liz West**: 218. **Pamela V. White**: 196. **Wikipedia**/Acroterion: 106, 148; Archi0780: 233; Beerguy721: 180; Beyondmyken: 121, 130; Daderot: 128, 136; Ebyabe: 112; Esetena: 138; Evybe: 112; Leaflet: 232; Mcheath: 188; Mwanner: 170; Sardaka: 152; Sysop: 104; Teemu08: 190.